The Annesley Drawings

The Annesley Drawings

DAVID ANNESLEY

Exile Editions, Toronto 1980

This edition is published by Exile Editions Limited,
20 Dale Avenue, Toronto, Ontario, Canada M4W 1K4

Sales Distribution:
McArthur & Company
c/o Harper Collins
1995 Markham Road
Toronto, ON
M1B 5M8
toll free:
1 800 387 0117
1 800 668 5788 (fax)

Original Design by *Tim Inkster*
Composed at *Moons of Jupiter,* Toronto
Printed and Bound by *Marc Veilleux Imprimeur,* Quebec

The publisher wishes to acknowledge
the assistance toward publication of the Canada Council
and the Ontario Arts Council.

The Canada Council
Conseil des Arts du Canada

ISBN 1-55096-551-4

Introduction

David Annesley was tall, bony and sandy-haired. He had a long face, wide-open yearning eyes, and slightly crooked teeth that gave a crooked gaiety to his shy laughter. It was the shy laughter of a man watching carefully, a country man's wariness. He was from the country, the town of Strabane in County Tyrone, the second son of Ulster protestants. His father had hired Catholics as scrub labor and was hard on them, but David was not hard, and had no prejudice, no religion. He'd left his home, footloose, and he'd had his fancy, but he was by no means free. He'd always wanted to draw but the Belfast College of Art had turned him away. In 1963, he came to Canada and worked as postman, delivery boy and draftsman. He was a desultory worker, hating the nine-to-five life. He began drawing heads, hoping to get published somewhere and get out of the grind.

He walked into my office at the old *Toronto Telegram.* It was February of 1968. I was the literary editor, writing a long book review or a personal piece every Saturday. There were other reviews by other writers. The book section had its own character and needed distinctive drawings. David said he'd sold one drawing for eight dollars but it had never been published. He had a small portfolio. The drawings were a mish-mash of cartoon heads, but there was something I liked about his line, and about him, a sheepish lackadaisical laughter that belied his eagerness. Within a few weeks, he was on regular salary.

He soon found his style, his own line, an elegant cleaness sometimes fractured and frenetic. He fascinated me. Week after week, he drew the heads of writers and politicians and yet seemed to have little or no interest in their ideas. There was only once that he asked about a writer's moral world. It was François Mauriac, and he was working from a grainy, dull photograph. I told him Mauriac made me think of a driven stake in the heart. 'I know about that,' he said, and drew Mauriac with a head hewn down to a point, but such talk was uncommon. By and large, he kept a distance between himself and the play of ideas. He almost never drew from life and seldom saw his subjects. If faces, as he drew them, had a character, it was because he tried to find the essential structure of the bones. He was interested in line. He had no moral and satirical axe to grind, no political point to make. He thought cross-hatching was clutter. One day, when I showed him a book of drawings by Matisse, he said full of excitement, 'They're like water.' It was a way of saying something about himself: he wanted to look at a face with as little clutter between his eye and the object as possible, and for him, emotion was clutter, muddied waters. With few exceptions, emotional involvement in his drawings led to confusion and cartoons.

I thought this was why, until the years close to his death, he could not draw women. He could draw ugly and older women like George Eliot or Golda Meir, but the rest he rendered as blank-faced starlets, cartoons devoid of personality and presence. We talked only a little about women, and he was a great womanizer, but he seemed burdened by a fear and sometimes a contempt for them. All this was blurred by a boyish awkwardness. When we talked, it was usually in my office at the newspaper, which was in the library, an office partitioned off by shoulder-high, pebble-glass walls. I kept cognac in a drawer, and there was always rowdy music from a portable record-player: Otis Spann, Junior Wells and Muddy Waters. Very few reporters came into the library. There was a glossy photograph of a naked, big-bosomed girl taped to the glass wall over the typewriter. We were talking about the face of James T. Farrell.

'You know her?' he said suddenly, eagerly.

'Yes,' I said.

'Her nipples are too big, they're no good.' He blushed. 'But I love big breasts.'

He was a loner who found women difficult and was difficult with women. It was not until he was divorced after an early and almost immediately unhappy marriage that he began to work well with color, and his drawings of women's faces – like that of Joyce Carol Oates – took on an energy and life. But his drawings of the naked body remained trite.

The confusion between us was more understandable, easier to explain. It came out of our working nights together. There was a big white-topped table on the other side of my pebble-glass wall. Sitting at the typewriter, drifting through my own stalled thoughts, I could see his shadow hunched like a big-boned bird, and sometimes he would get up and circle and shuffle, upset and fed-up because he couldn't capture a likeness, and one night, the first time he tried to draw Philip Roth, he cursed and handed me his drawing. It was three in the morning.

'It won't do,' I said.

'I can't do any better.'

'You must.'
'I won't.'
'You must.'
'I will, and fuck you.'
'You're right.'
'About what?'
'Do it again.'
'No.'
'You must.'

A certain closeness grew between us, and every year he tried a drawing of me, wanting to give me a gift. But the drawings never looked like me. His line was full of uncertainty, and at last, blushing, he tore them up and said, 'I can't draw anyone like you knowing you like I do.'

On one occasion, however, his angry confusion gave him a very good drawing. It followed a mid-afternoon lunch I'd had with the visiting Irish poet, John Montague, who'd been brought up as a Catholic in Ulster. We were in the office having a drink and listening to music. The door opened. David, with his crooked boyish smile, stepped in. Montague cocked his head and cried playfully, 'I smell a Prot.' David turned red, stammered, and then stood silently and furiously staring at the floor. Montague, a man of mischievous wit, needled and stitched his countryman. There was no animosity on Montague's part; only the prickliness of the place they came from. David fumed, and later we all went to supper. He was not up to the verbal play, and afterwards, he stormed and stomped.

'I won't draw him. I can't,' he insisted.
'You must.'
'I won't.'

But he did, and brought in the drawing, flushed with satisfaction. He'd given Montague a pursed mouth, a chicken neck and empty eyes. It was unkind and cruel, and yet the twisted lines told a truth.

His talent, his ability to take hold of a face's truth, got him into trouble among men who were not so good humored as Montague. He'd done, for example, a wonderful whimsical Marshall McLuhan, a face appropriate to puns and metaphysical probes. To David's delight and surprise, he got a call from McLuhan, asking him to come around to the Centre and David, always pressed for money, hoped for a sale. But for some reason he did not take the drawing along, and when McLuhan asked for it, he said, No ... he had not brought it. McLuhan told him he was lucky, that he hated it, and he'd hoped to tear it up in his face. David was shown out of the famous office with the Cambridge oar on the wall, chastened and bewildered. He was still short of money that week because he existed on what he was paid at the *Telegram.* That was only fifty dollars, which the senior editors regularly tried to cut back to thirty-five, and when, in my last year with the paper, I gave him seventy-five, a senior editor said to me, somewhat prophetically, 'Here's your hat, what's your hurry.' Too often, David had to depend on such men.

It was partly this problem of money, but I think it was more David's nature that he settled where he did, in an abandoned brick school house outside the country town of Beaverton. He was, after all, a country man who liked to work with his hands, and he was expert at castrating pigs. He did a lot of carpentry, digging and haying, and he began to try sculpture. There was a lovely river a short walk from the house. He felt calmed beside the river and, for a man so tied to the whims of editors, it was strange that he had no telephone. In the winter, with drifting snow closing the roads, he was often shut in and untroubled by it. Obviously, he was self-sufficient and took satisfaction at being alone with himself so many days on end.

But there were times, such as the night I wrote about Auden or the night John Steinbeck died, when someone had to be phoned who drove around to him in the dark and then he drove down to the early morning city.

These were our closest working moments, separated by the pebble-glass wall, shadows of each other as we tried to get hold of the right line, the right word. He showed me his drawing, I read my piece aloud, and then took them down to the composing room.

He was suspicious of that room because some of the men and women were quite peculiar, one woman sometimes so drunk she wore her dress backwards and there was a man who refused to set deadline type unless he was fed free chinese food. But more unsettling was the fact that someone was stealing his originals. It was a constant problem for him, not only at the *Telegram,* but later when he sold some drawings to *The Globe and Mail.* He told me they had treated him shabbily and lost several originals and when he tried to charge them, they told him to get lost. He did not work for them again.

He did well enough, however, locally and internationally, appearing in many magazines, among them the *New York Times,* the *Atlantic,* the *National Review, The New Yorker,* and *Saturday Night.* He was more and more excited by working with color, and sometime before he died, he made a leap in self-esteem. He stopped signing his drawings. He was at last convinced that his line in itself was his signature. He was in his stride, ready to make new discoveries, but he died young, drowning in the Gulf of Mexico at the age of thirty-three. He was buried on a cold rainy day in February of 1977 in a country graveyard.

The Annesley Drawings

Golda Meir

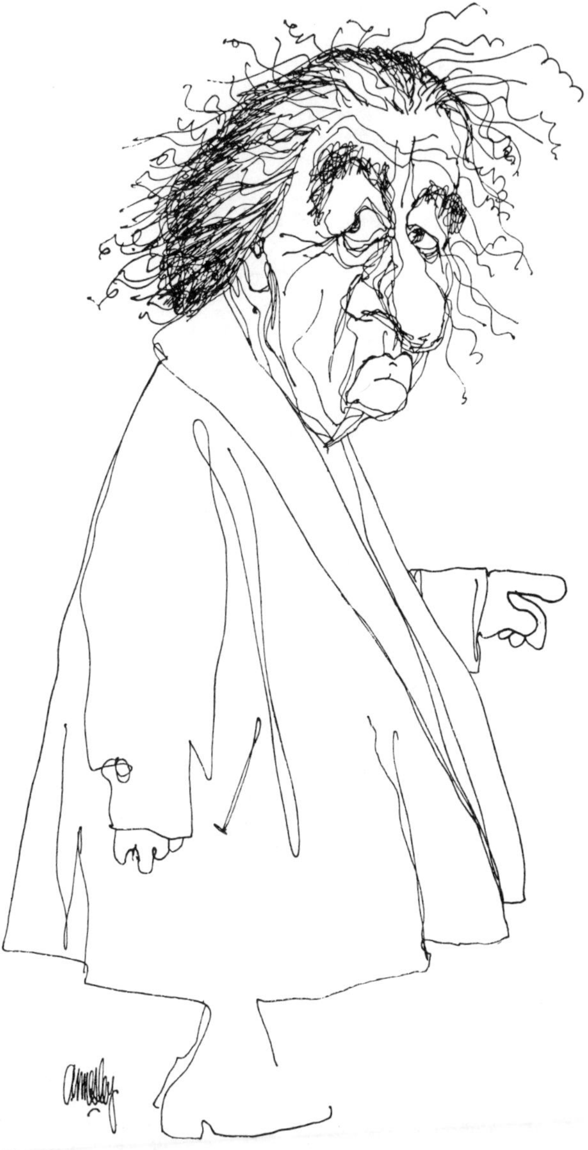

Philip Roth

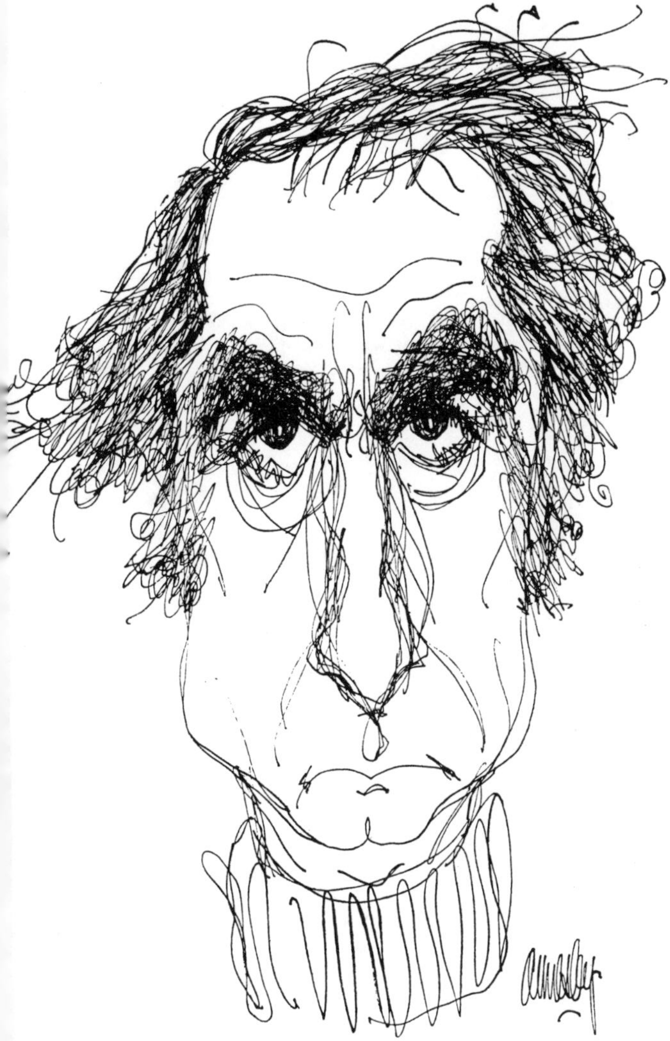

Jerzy Kosinsk

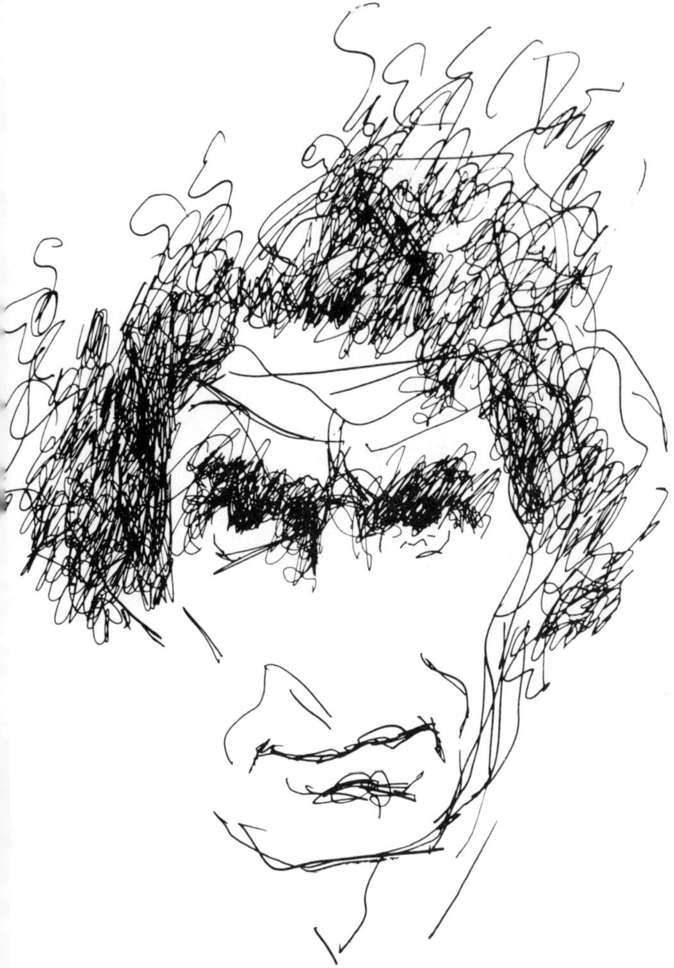

Mordecai Richler

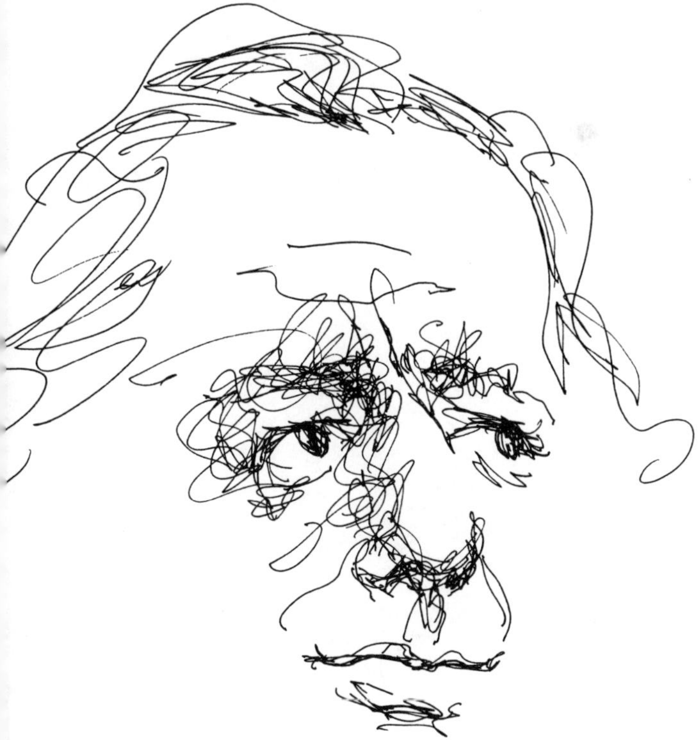

George Elio

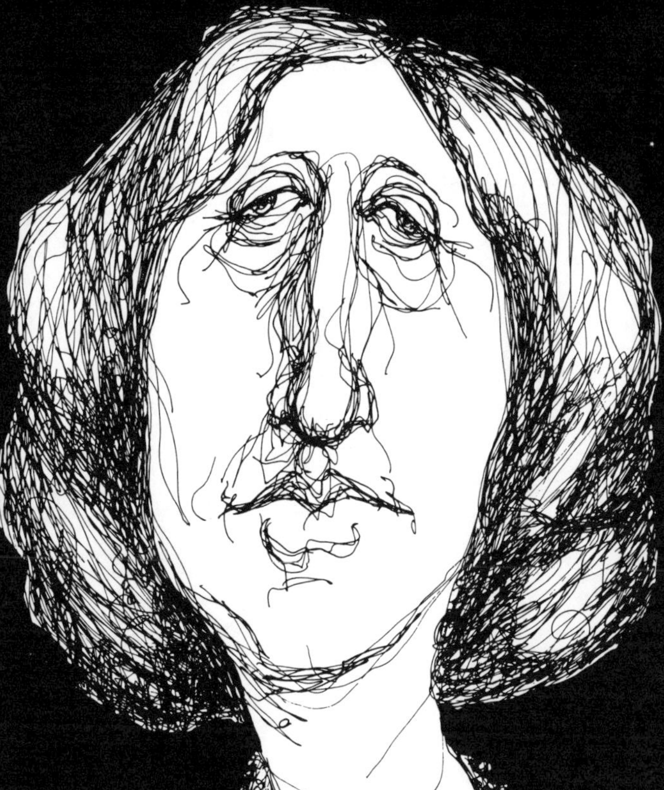

François Mauriac

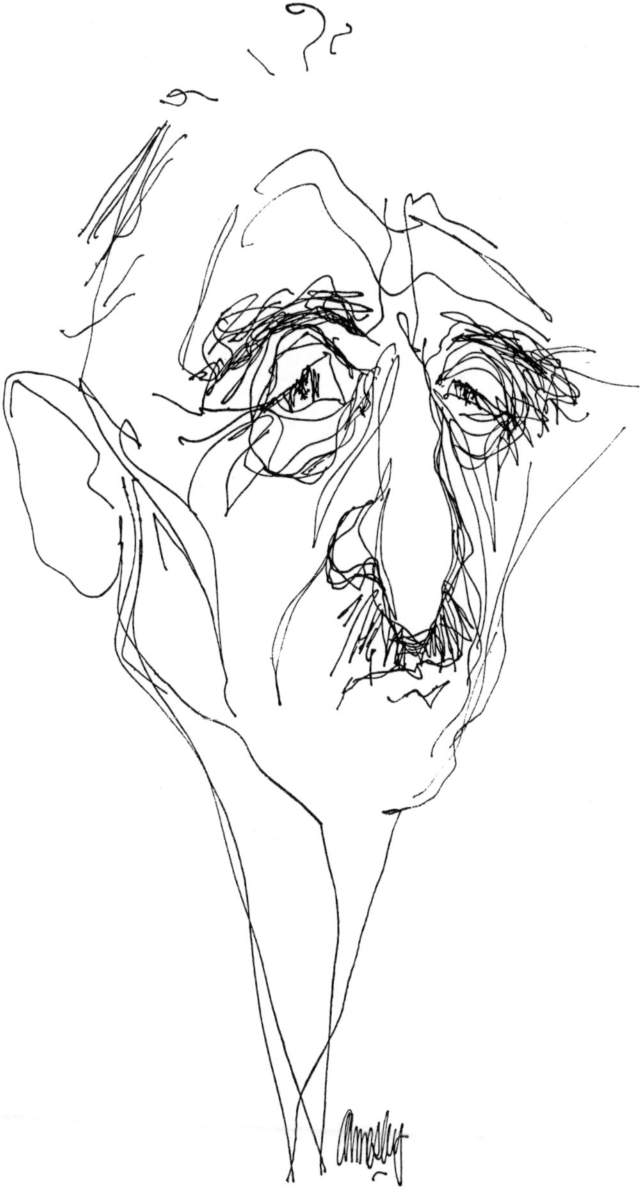

Ezra Pound

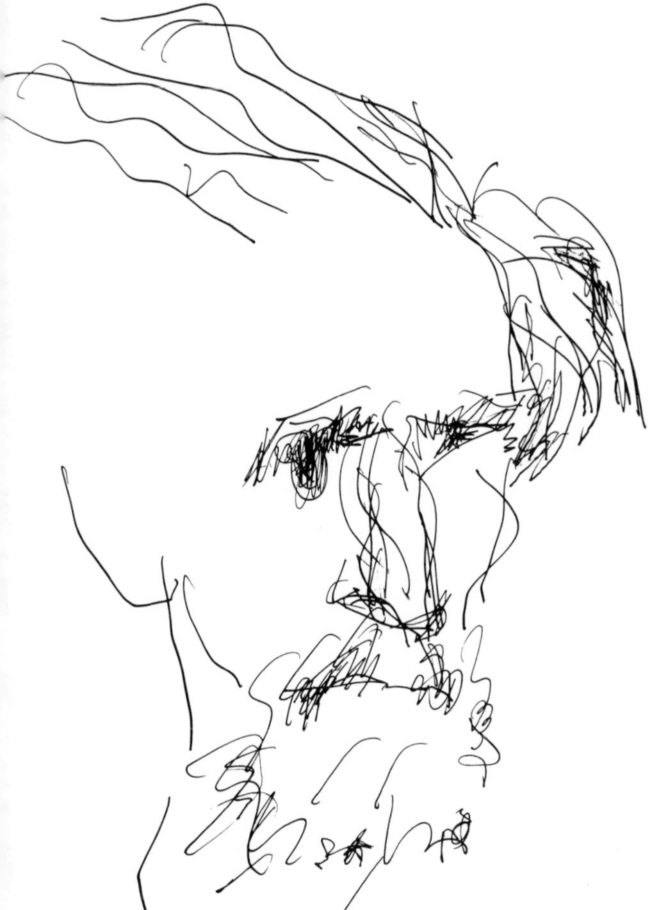

Celine

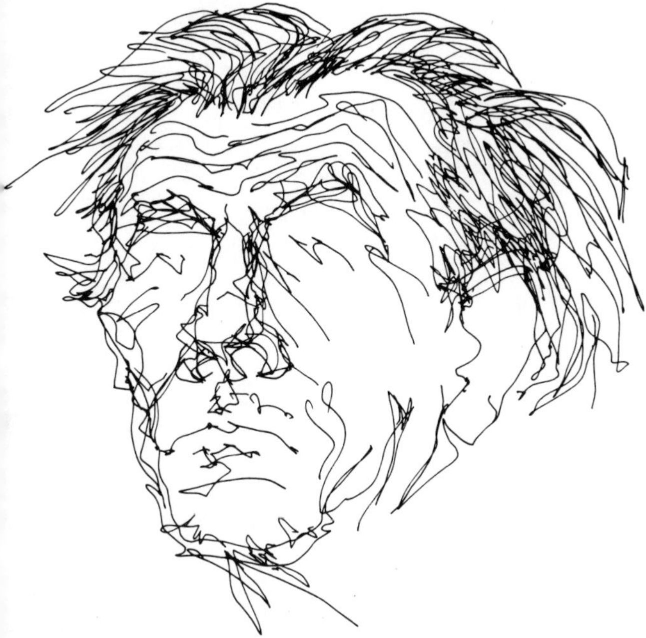

John Montagu

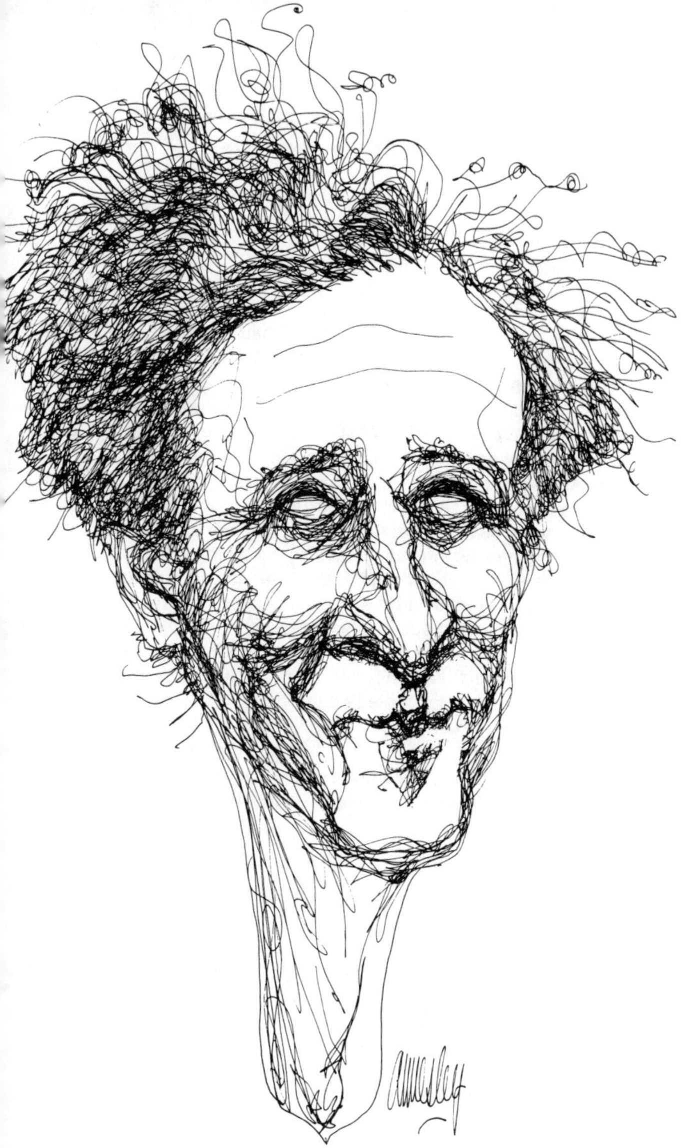

W. H. Auden was much taller than I had expected, heavier, and long-armed, and there were pouches under his eyes and intricate web-lines in his brow. His voice was low, a sing-song, broken in rhythms set to some inner machine, clicking away, and between poems he appealed to his wrist-watch, his lips moving, as if counting down the seconds allowed for breathing space.

At a verbal gaff, he hurled back his arms and head in laughter, except there was no sound from him; only the wide gape of his mouth, as in one of Goya's screaming women, except there was no sound and he was laughing, slapping his thighs with his long arms.

He read one of his poems about his house outside Vienna, a house once owned by a great Austrian poet who committed suicide. His tone was one of sadness, methodical, a nostalgia for dogs and gardens and banisters and chairs and a light that once was and friends lost and friends alive in memory, kept alive in his curious knocking rhythms that clicked off the years, the rooms, time passed.

There was a certain gaiety about him, his love of puzzles and word tricks and an urbanity of wit that would please a Pope, whether he was in a London coffeehouse or the Vatican. A good deal of this, of course, was merely cute, made up of little drawing room jokes:

Joseph Hayden
Never read Dryden;
John Dryden
Never heard Hayden.

It was the sadness, never the leap of the imagination into the unknown, but the sadness surrounding the bric-a-brac of life, the tables, the chairs, the friends once had, flattened to the scale, whether sordid or elegant, of the room and then another room that touched me about Auden, and then the playing out of precise emotions in those rooms where his men and women never seemed larger than they were but were compelled by an order ordained, something hard and unyielding beneath the tone.

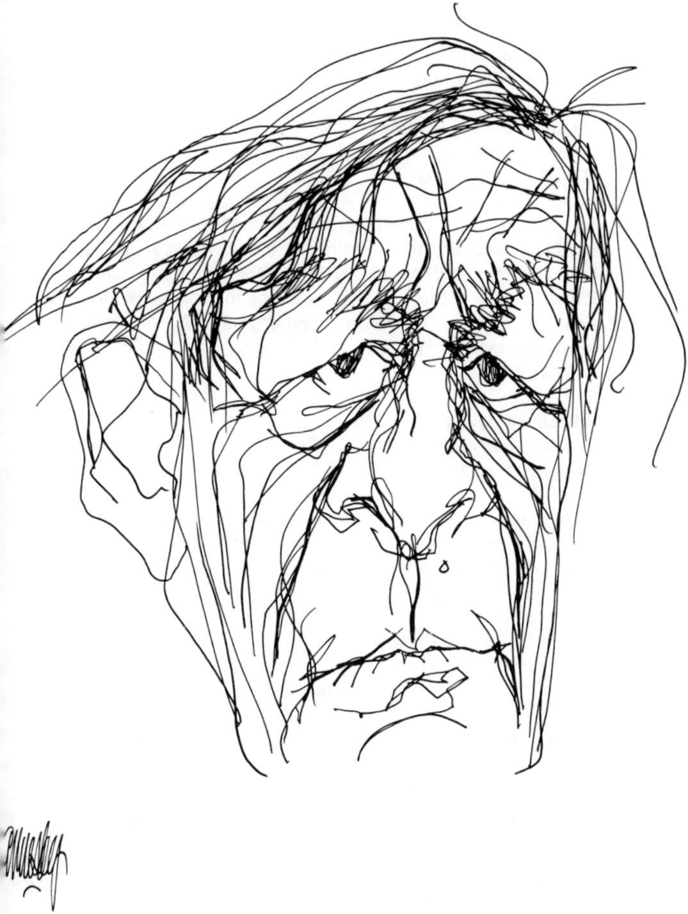

There was a certain sharpness in him, a sharp distilling of words into the stiletto of aphorism:

A dead man
Who never caused others to die
Seldom rates a statue.

In semi-literate countries
Demagogues pay
Court to teen-agers.

A coldness, and something astringent about these aphorisms. The grand sweep of men's emotions and motives was diminished to a sharp saying, to a deft touch of scorn, and surely this came out of a distrustful view of the world, this wanting to reduce men to a witty phrase. But then, this was not altogether true of Auden. Among the great maxim-makers, he was a maverick, a man touched in his severity by pity:

When we do evil,
We and our victims
Are equally bewildered.

It seemed, for Auden, to be a question of perspective. An evil world of evil men: men bewildered in a bewildering world: pitiable, and perhaps not beyond redemption:

O look, look in the mirror,
    O look in your distress;
Life remains a blessing
    Although you cannot bless.

There was a dreadful, touching aloneness in those lines. Whatever was going on is going on no matter the distress of the face in the mirror, no matter the good will, no matter the hatred. (Auden said: "By all means let a poet, if he wants to, write engagé poems, protesting against this or that political evil or social injustice. But let him remember this: The only person who will benefit from them is himself; they will enhance his literary reputation among those who feel as he does. The evil or injustice, however, will remain exactly what it would have been if he had kept his mouth shut.")

Evil or injustice or indifference, or even that cold impersonal blessing, these have no ending; but love and the reaching for the sun, these have an ending, the human cry soon forgotten:

...Icarus for instance: how everything turns away
Quite leisurely from the disaster; the ploughman may
Have heard the splash, the forsaken cry,
But for him it was not an important failure; the sun shone
As it had to on the white legs disappearing into the green
Water, and the expensive delicate ship that must have seen
Something amazing, a boy falling out of the sky,
Had somewhere to get to and sailed calmly on.

But then, this cruel sense of calm indifference was not the whole of Auden (He said: "We are not commanded [or forbidden] to love our mates, our children, our friends, our country, because such affections come naturally to us and are good in themselves, although we may corrupt them. We are commanded to love our neighbour because our 'natural' attitude toward the 'other' is one of either indifference or hostility."):

O stand, stand at the window
As the tears scald and start;
You shall love your crooked neighbour
With all your crooked heart.

It was a command, not from an evangelical preacher, but from, perhaps a worldly cardinal poised in his high-back chair who understood the order of such things—that Man is fallen and fallen low into bestiality, lying down with and even in love with his pigs, but at the edge of gloom, he did not slip. He knew—if he did not deeply feel—that God had become Man and had died for Man, and Auden observed this redemptive truth from his own ironic perspective, of course. (He said: "Just as we were all, potentially, in Adam when he fell, so we were all, potentially, in Jerusalem on that first Good Friday... It seems to me worthwhile asking ourselves who we should have been and what we should have been doing. None of us, I'm certain, will imagine himself as one of the disciples, cowering in an agony of spiritual despair and physical terror. Very few of us are big wheels enough to see ourselves as Pilate, or good churchmen enough to see ourselves as a member of the Sanhedrin. In my most optimistic mood I see myself as a Hellenized Jew from Alexandria visiting an intellectual friend. We are walking along, engaged in philosophical argument. Our path takes us past the base of Golgotha. Looking up, we see an all too familiar sight—three crosses surrounded by a jeering crowd. Frowning with prim distaste, I say, 'It's disgusting the way the mob enjoys such things. Why can't the authorities execute criminals humanely and in private by giving them hemlock to drink as they did with Socrates?' Then, averting my eyes from the disagreeable spectacle, I resume our fascinating discussion about the nature of the True, the Good, and the Beautiful.")

The irony, the unrelenting irony, leavened only by pity, by a certain urbane wit, by a willed love out of the crookedness of the heart. Christ, Icarus, they cry, they fall, and men are either eating or opening a window or just walking dully along, running their course, and as everything runs its course, so may everything be distilled to the stiletto of aphorism:

The decent, probably,
Outnumber the swine,
But few can inherit
The genes, or procure
Both the money and time,
To join the civilized.

As he read a last poem in memory of Mozart, I thought of his mouth, gaping wide in laughter, black, silent, and how Mauriac used to say that he always wished to write with the lightness of Mozart but when he took up his pen the dark angels bore in upon him. Auden's angels have always been a little grey about the wings for me, but they have been angels nonetheless. That was Auden's genius, his surpassing of chic and attitudes, the way he refused to let go, or perhaps more accurately, had allowed himself to be borne forward by his angels, imposing his own order, his own constant voice, his wit, his laughter, in the rooms and hallways and lanes and gardens.

Adolf Hitler

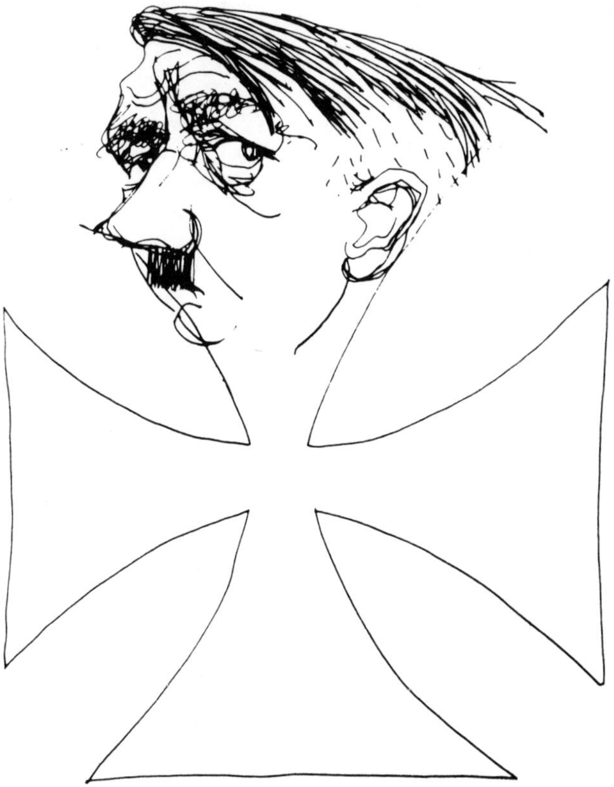

Frederick Phillip Grove

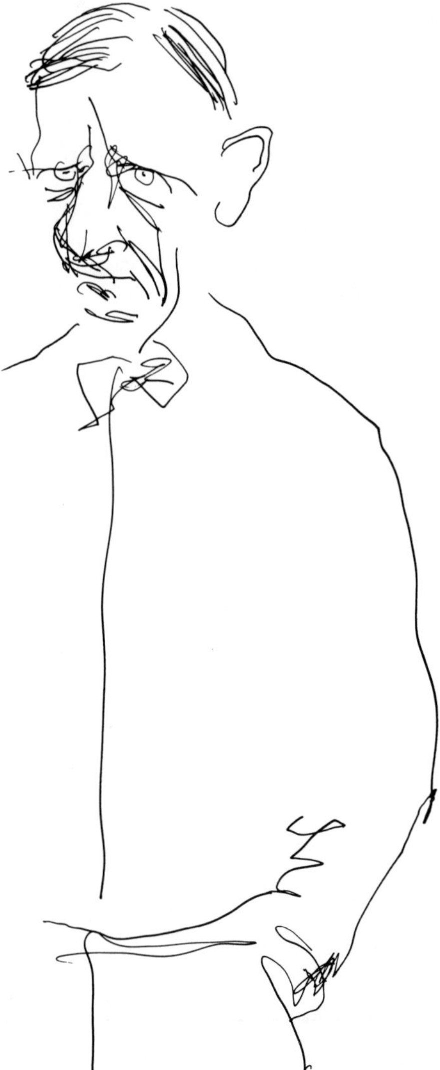

Morley Callaghan

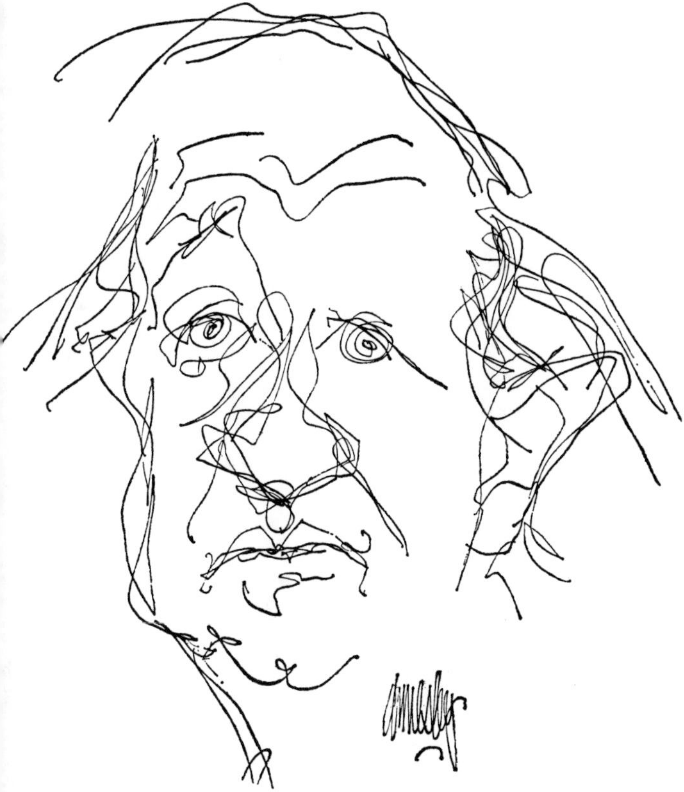

Brian Moore

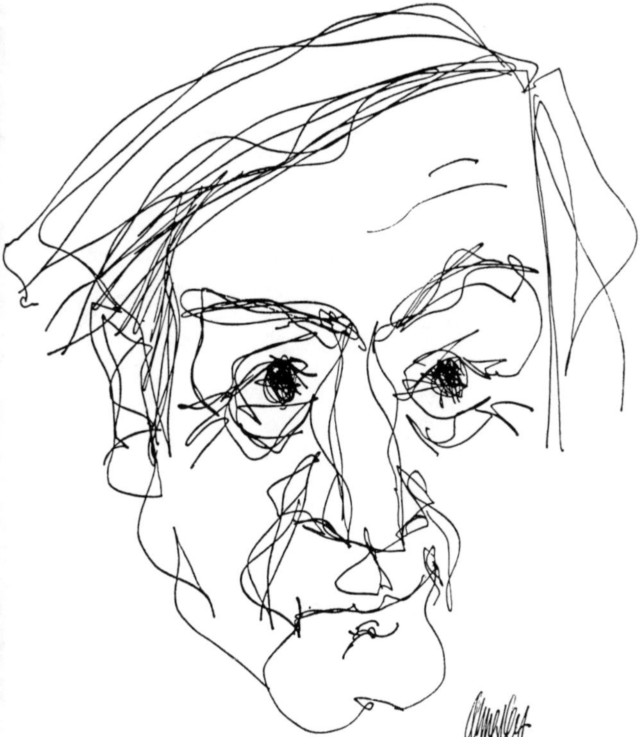

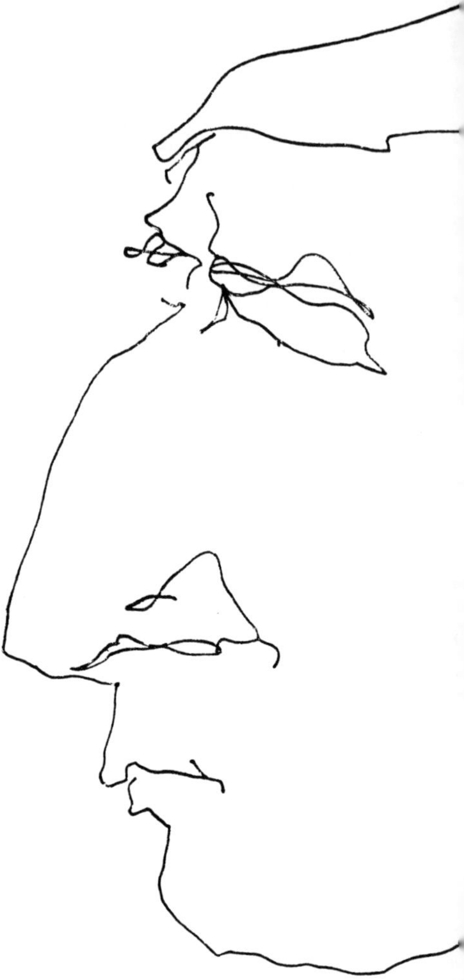

John Updike

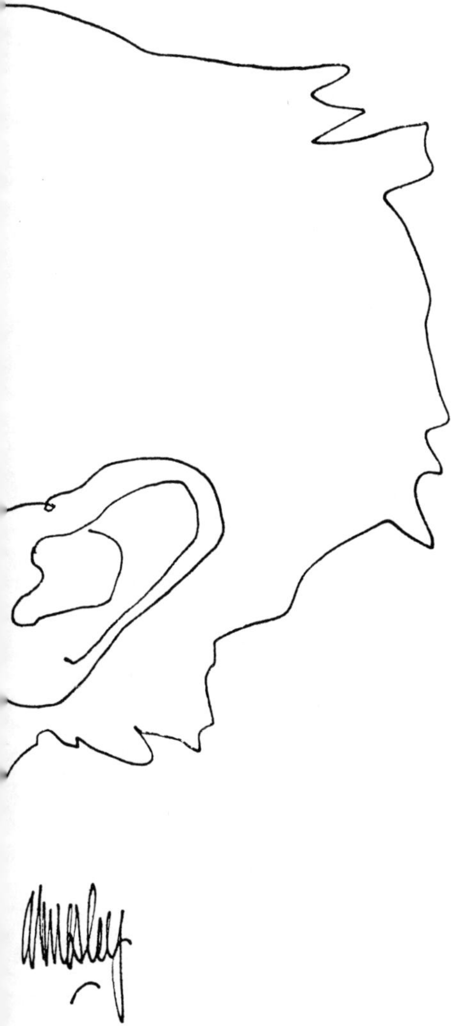

Irving Layton

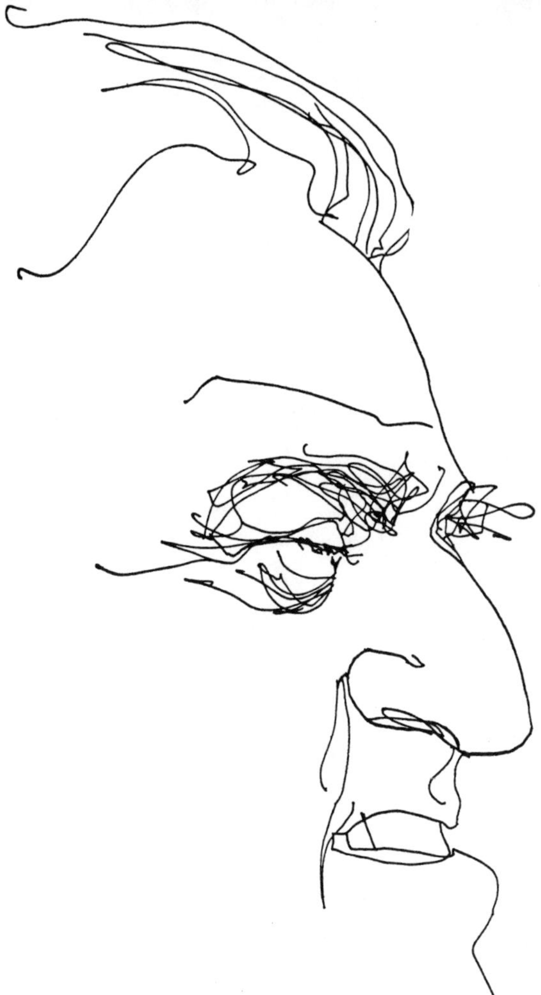

Austin Clarke

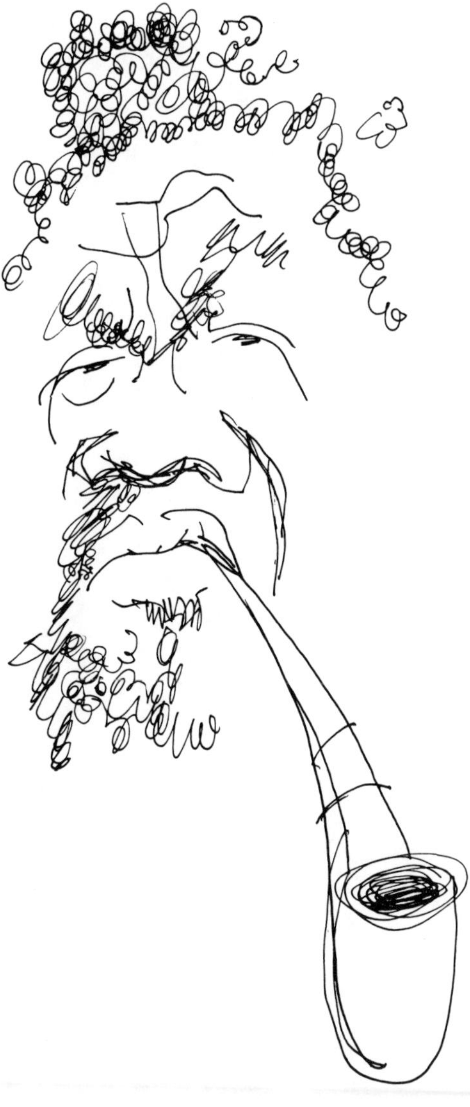

Gunter Grass

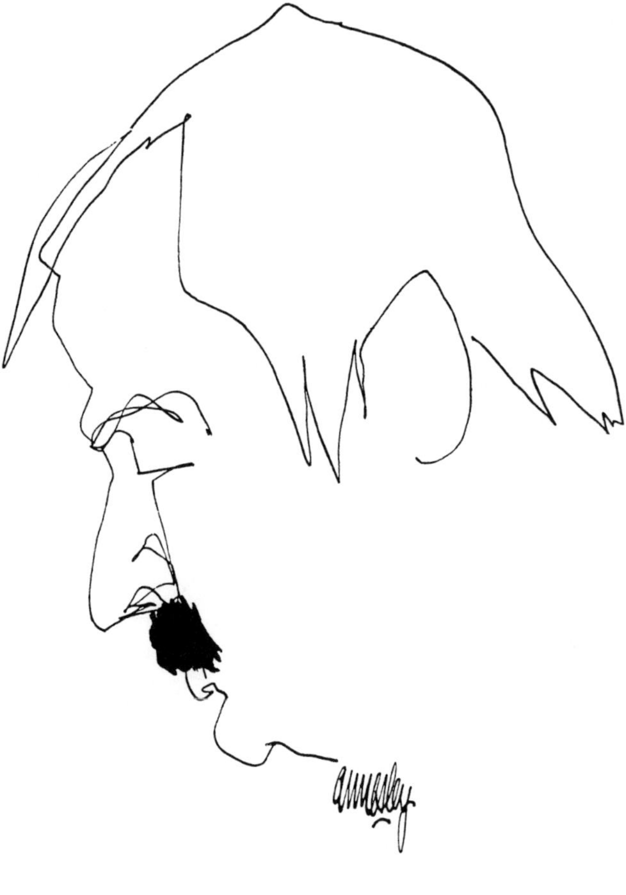

Ludwig von Beethoven

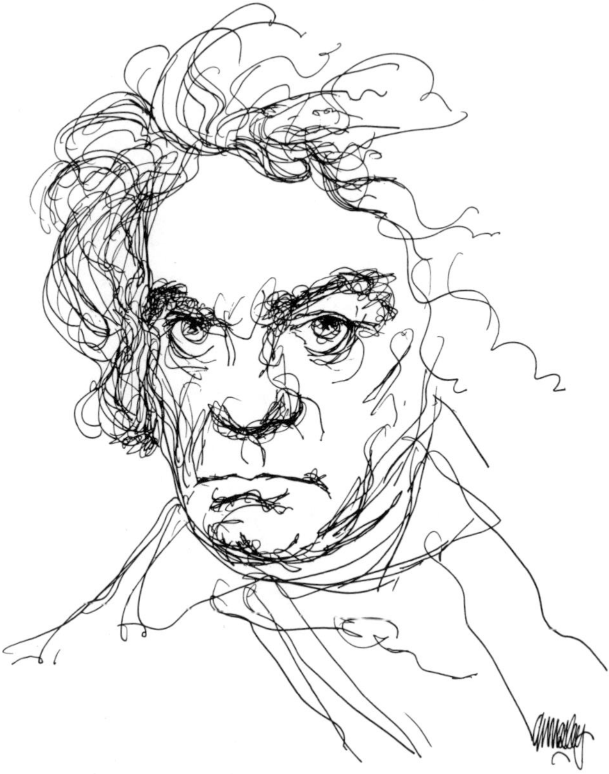

Johannes Brahms

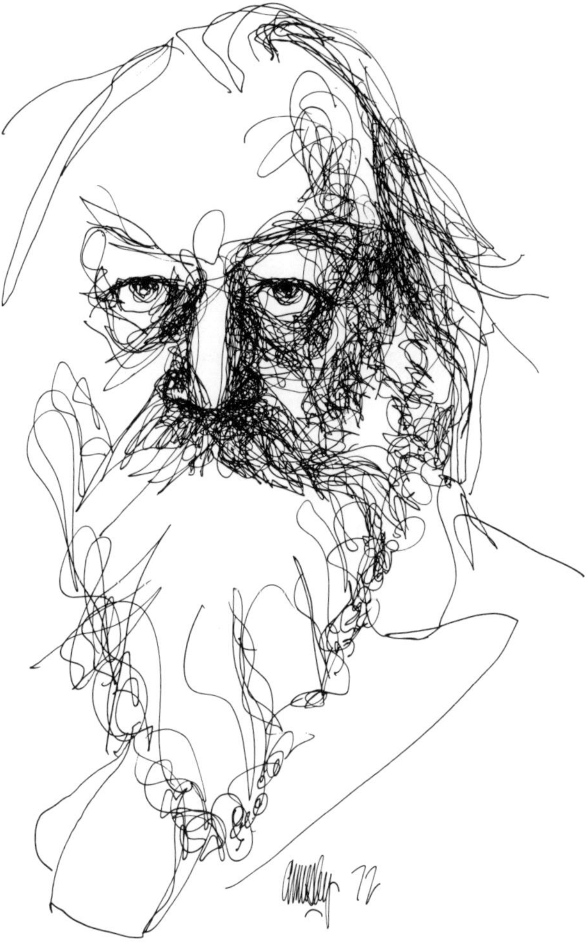

Robertson Davie

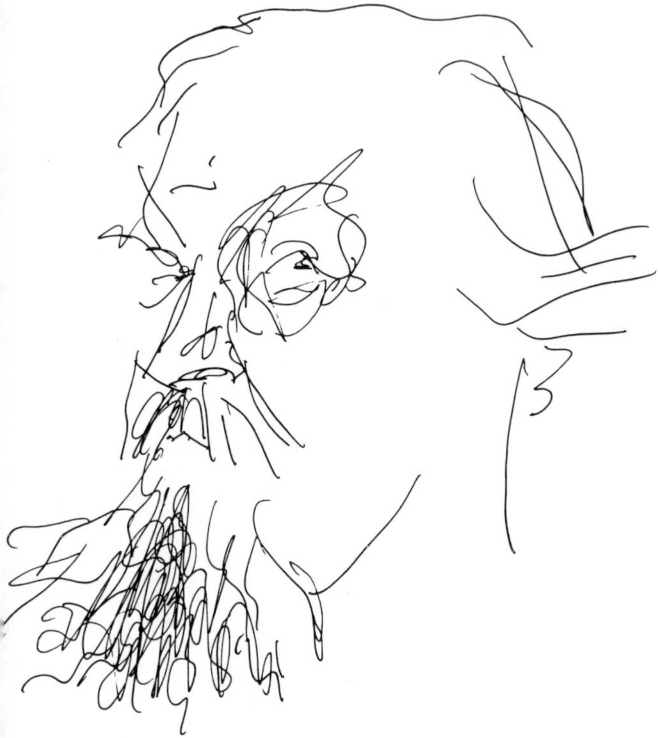

Generals W.C. Westmoreland and Tomayuki Yamashita

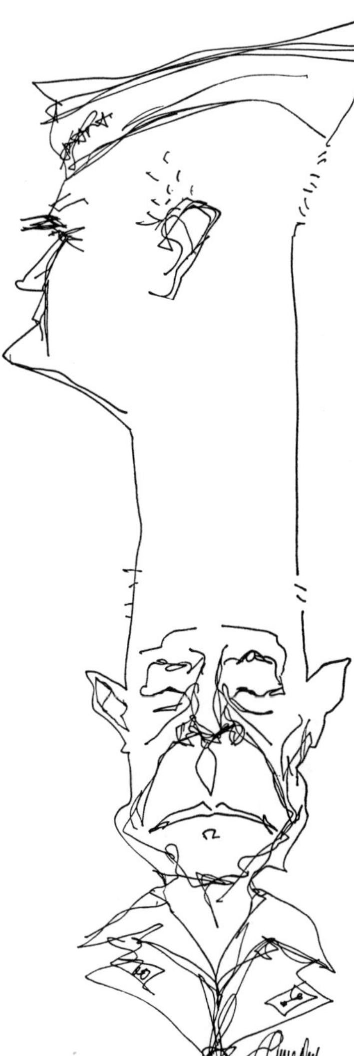

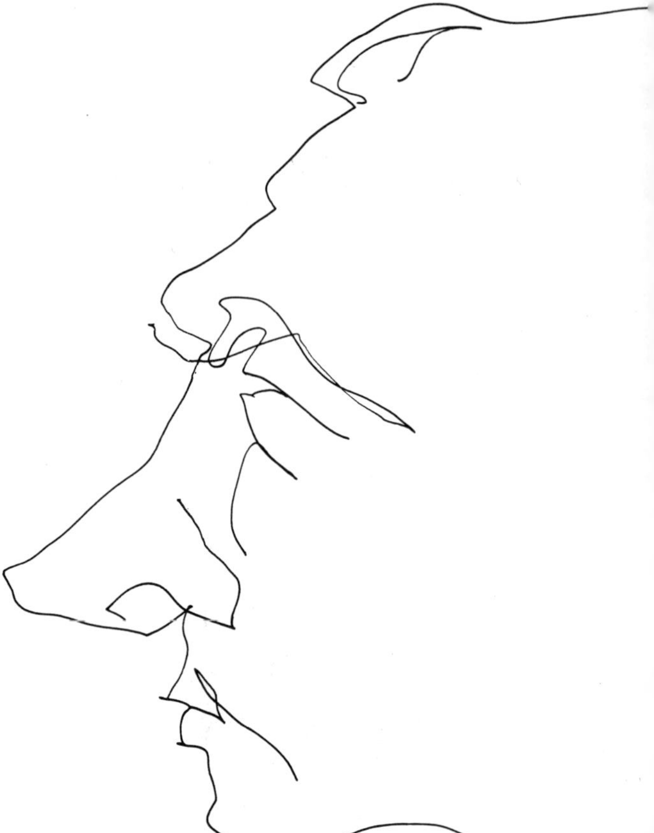

Saccho and Vanzetti

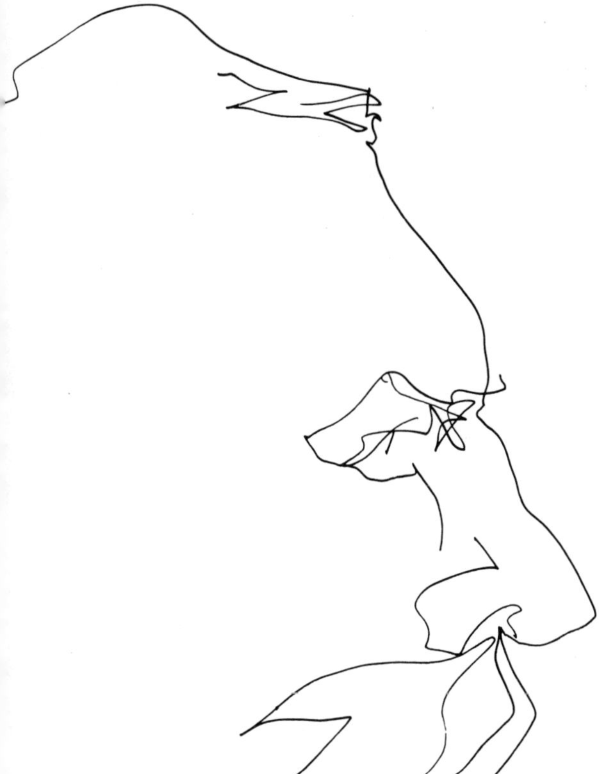

Ho Chi Minh

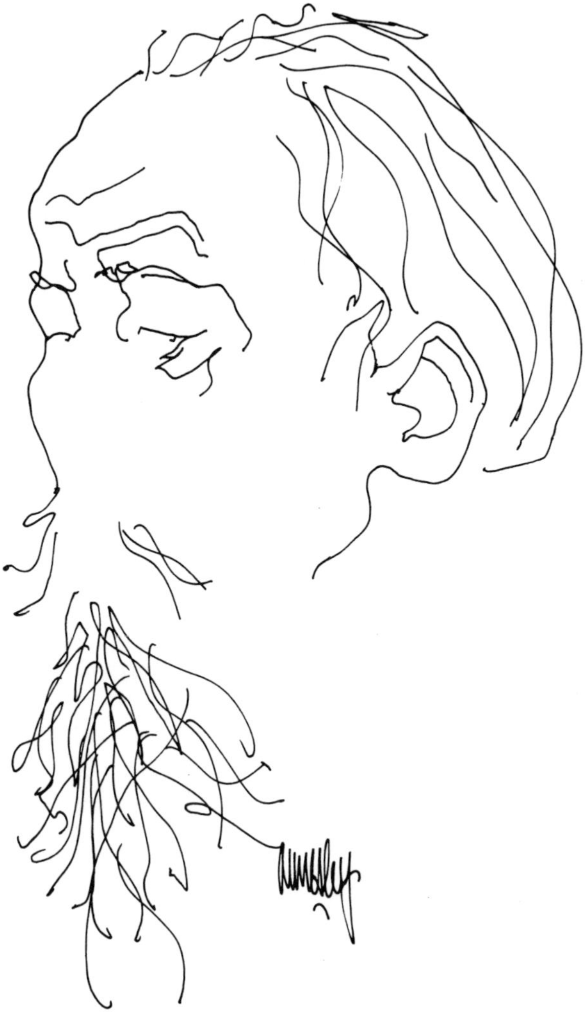

Nikita Khrushchev

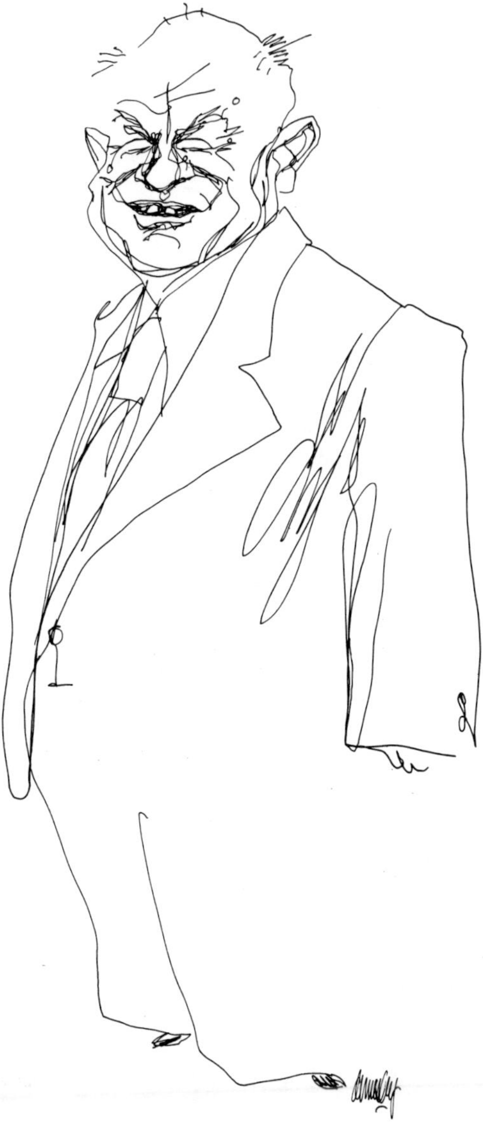

Pierre Elliot Trudeau

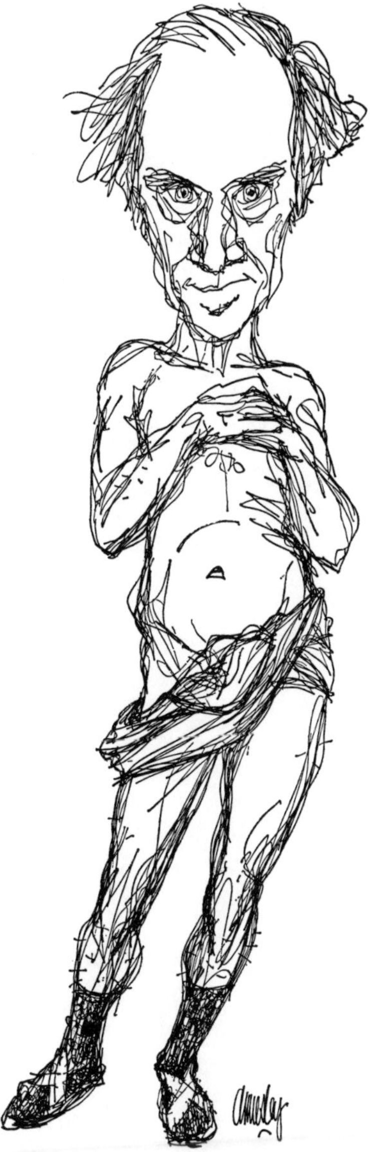

Sir John A. MacDonald

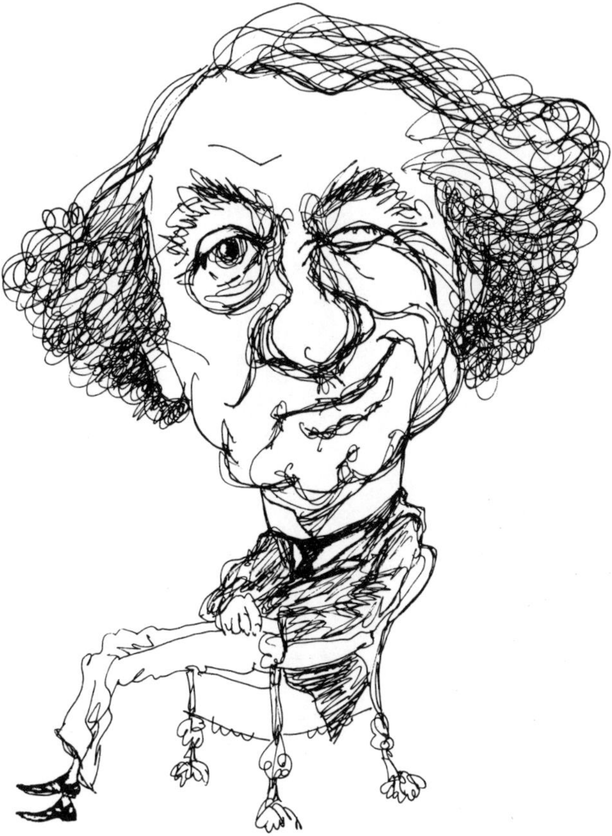

Gamal Abdul Nasse

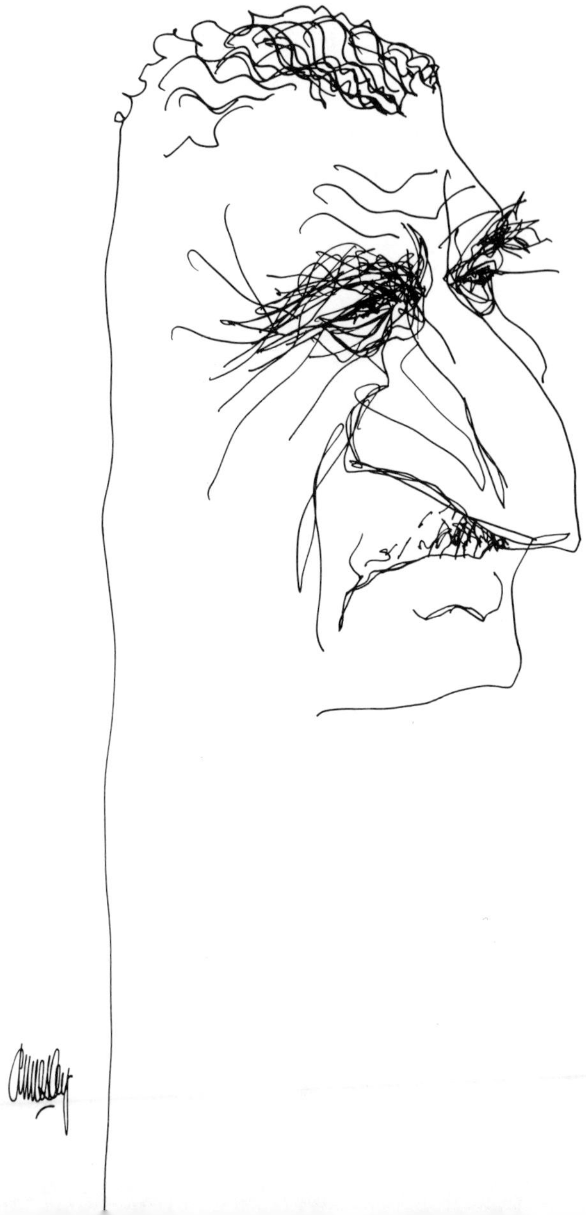

Charles de Gaulle

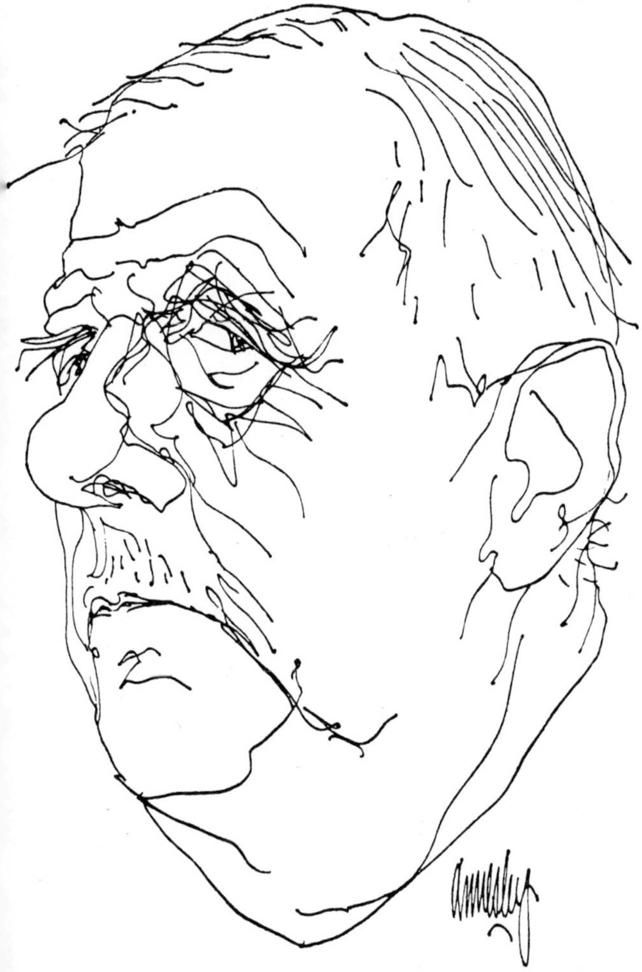

John Diefenbaker

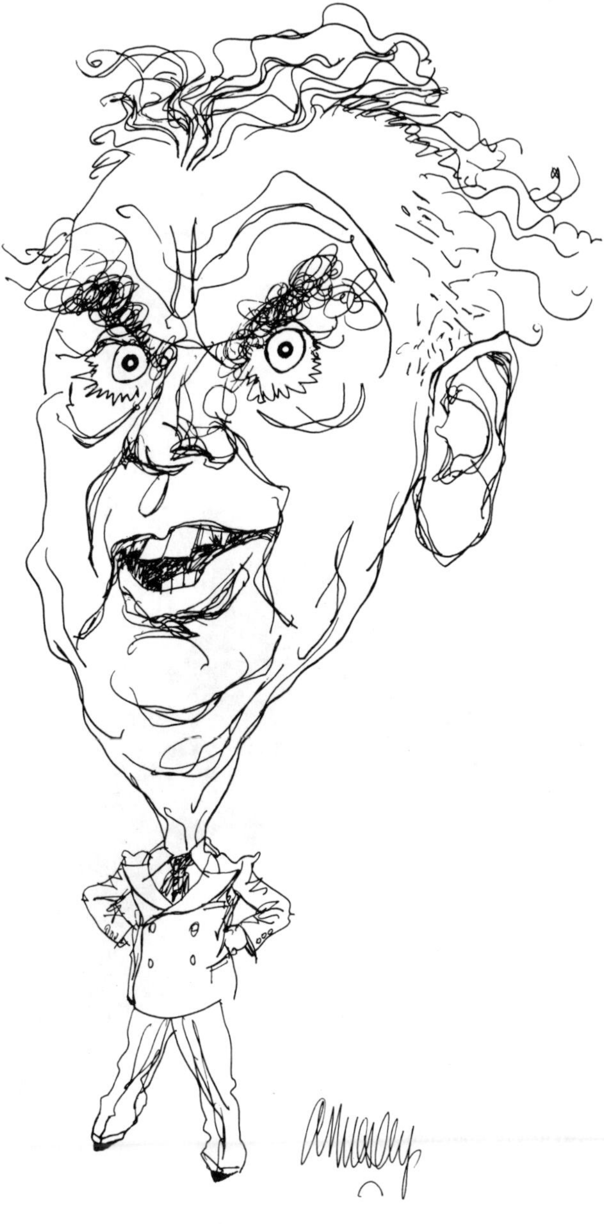

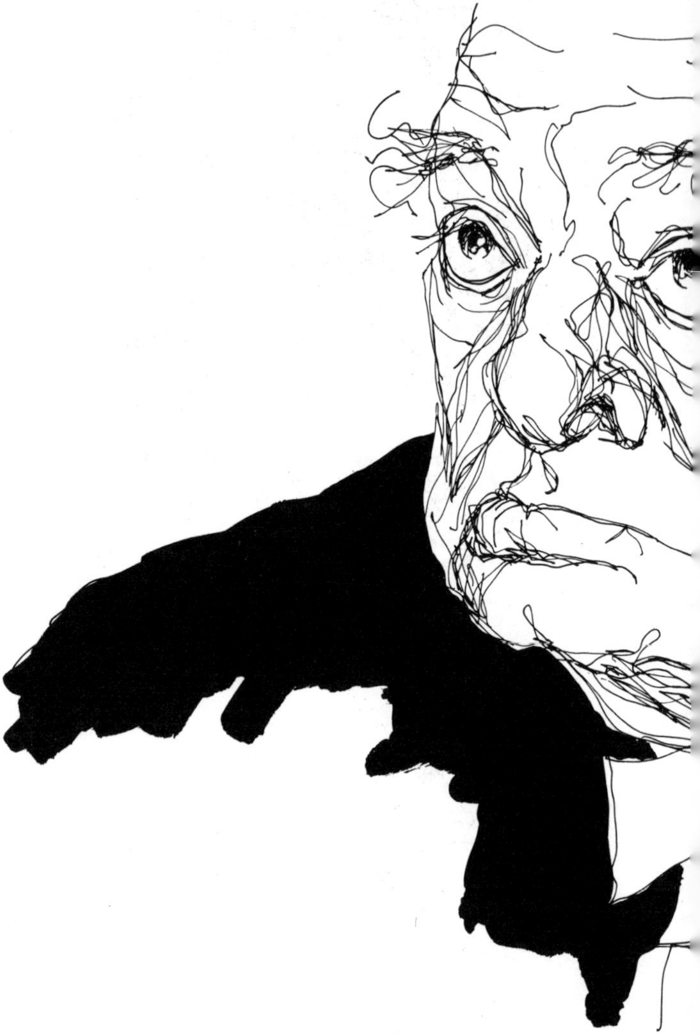

Winston Churchill

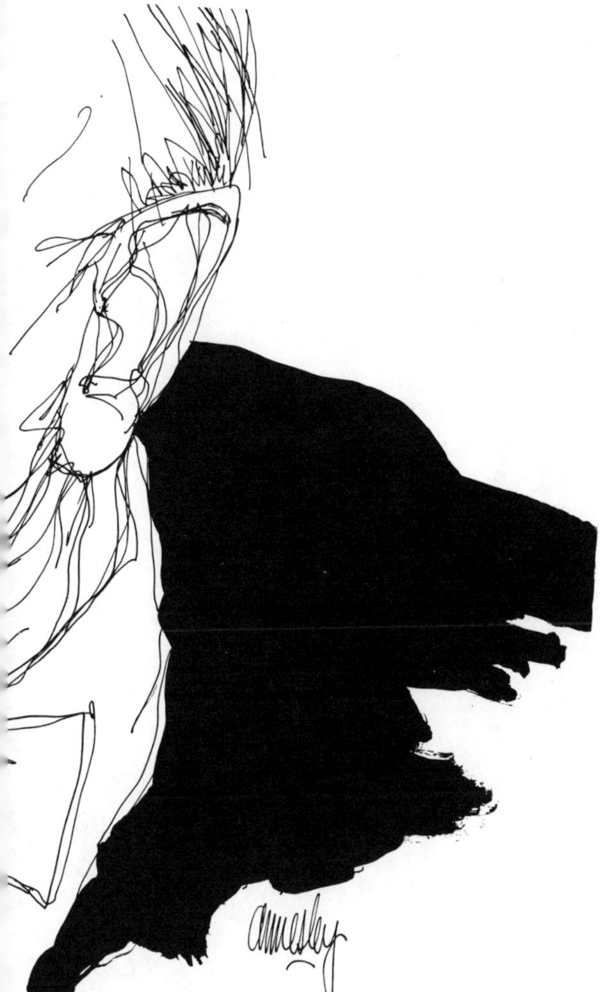

Bertrand Russe

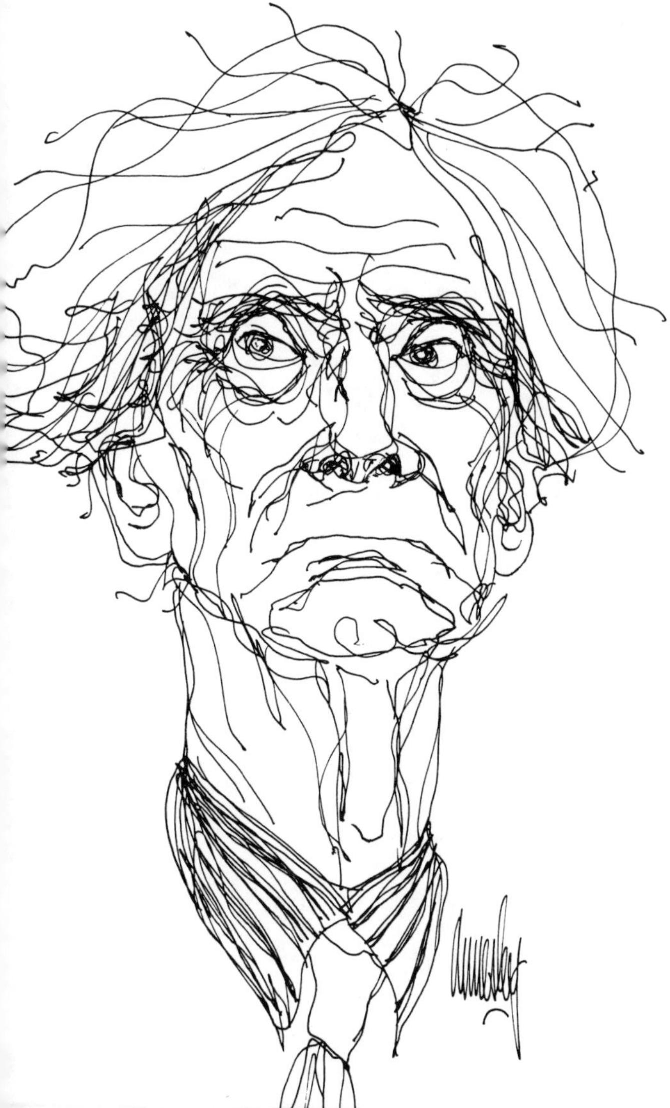

Samuel Beckett

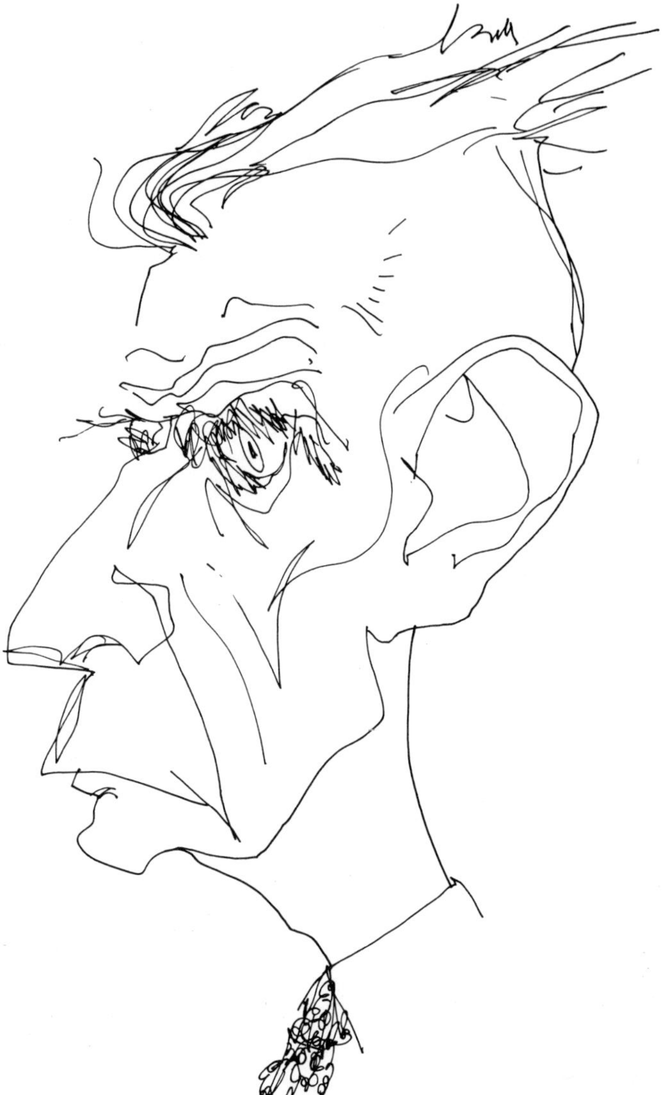

Jakov Lind

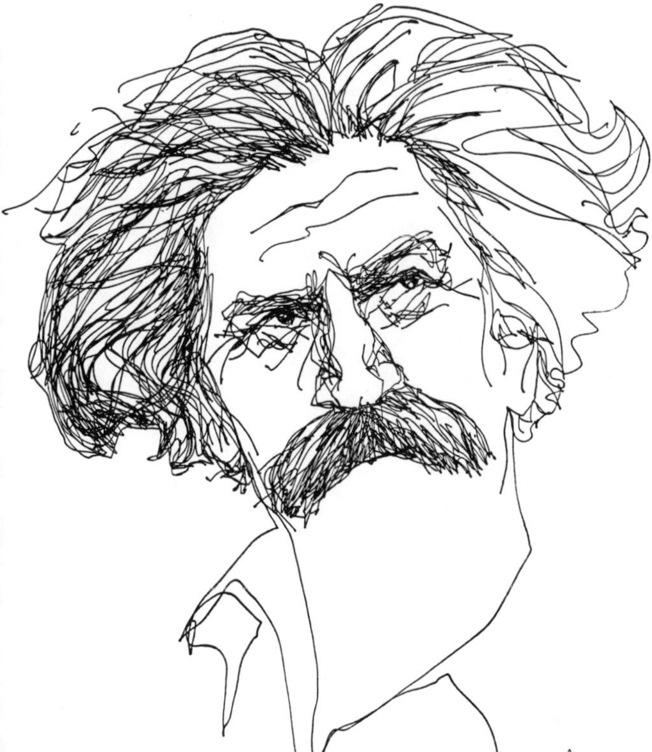

James Baldwi

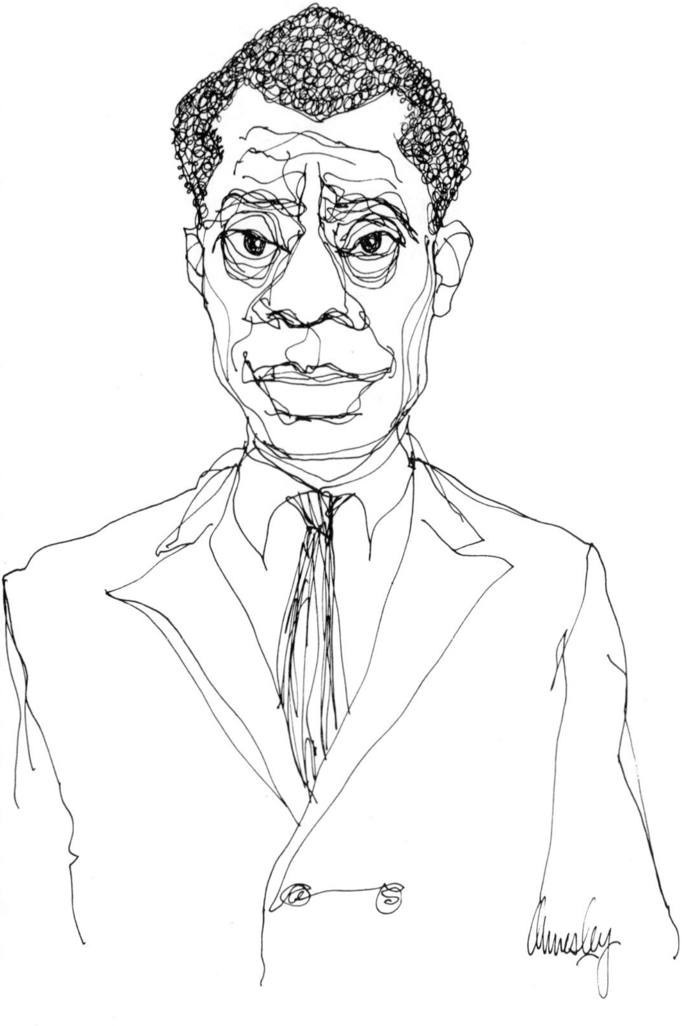

Dean Acheson

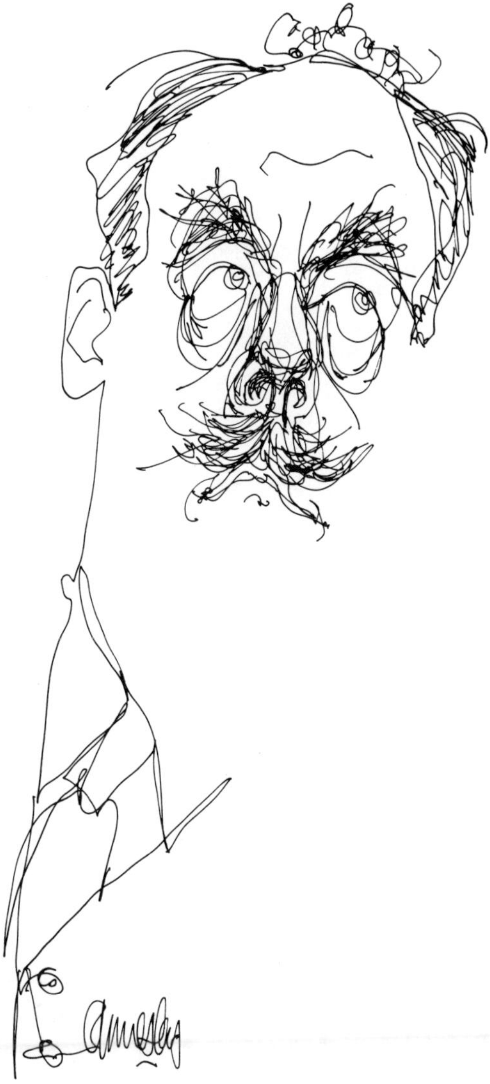

Muriel Spark

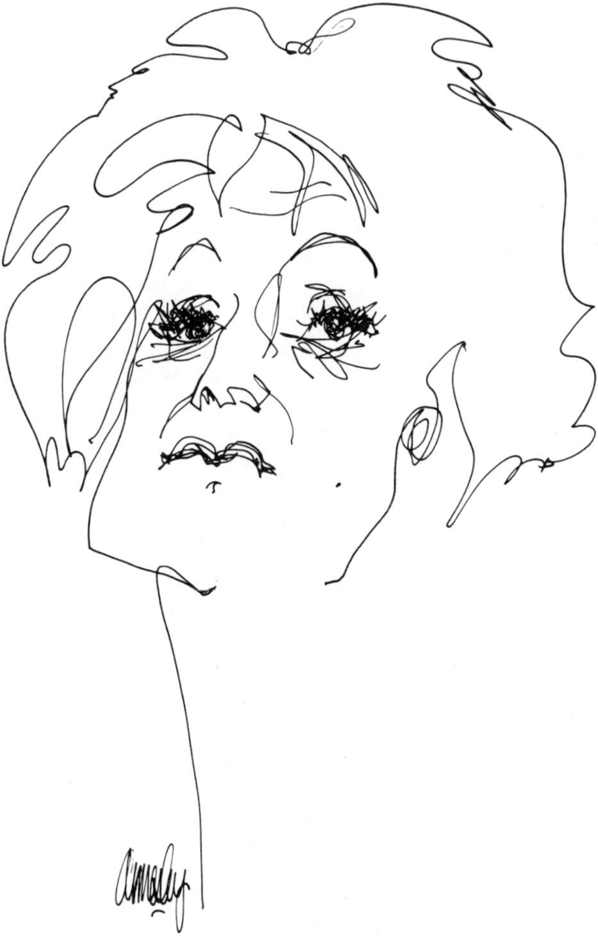

John Berryman

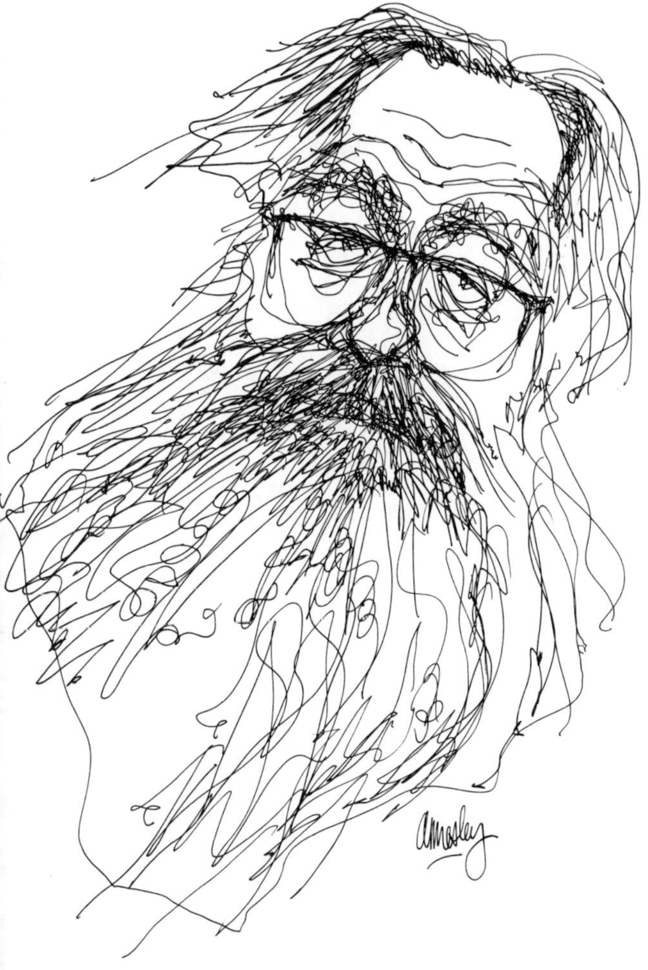

George Bernard Shaw

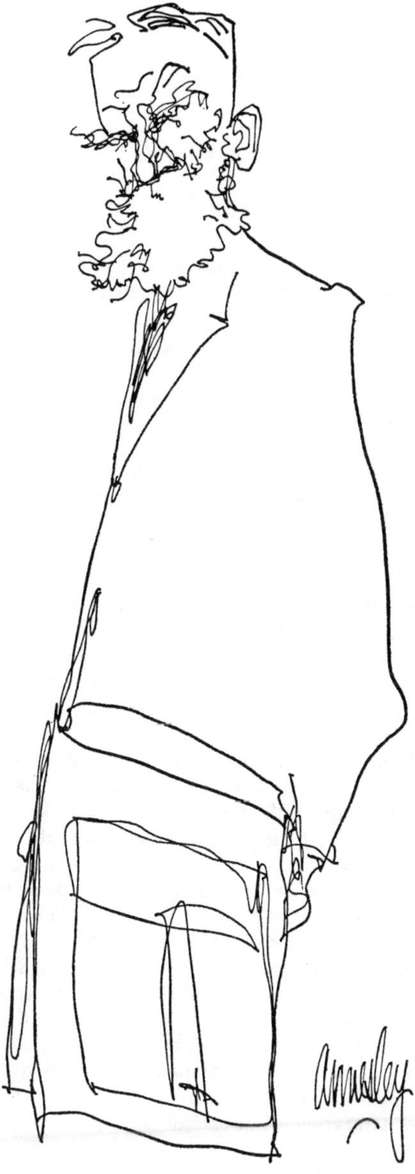

John Steinbeck has died. When I was a boy Steinbeck made me feel I had been around for a long year. I used to walk by rooming houses late at night in the summer and worn-out women in their cotton dresses used to sit on the front stoops drinking wine in the cool night air, and one night a woman with her stockings rolled at her calves said, 'Sit down boy and sip a while.' Later she said, 'Jesus, I crossed this whole damn country, just sipping here and sipping there ...' I said: 'You got the turtle in you,' and she said, 'Kid, I ain't seen a turtle since years ago ...'

I've always had the image of the turtle in my mind, Steinbeck's turtle, crawling and clawing and boosting his shell, his horny, dumb, amused head, crossing highways, pressing a few seeds inside his shell, and then a smart-ass trucker trying to run him down, catching the tail of the shell and flipping it into the air, but when it landed it scrambled on, dropping spearhead seeds in the ground, dragging dirt over the seeds, going on down a dust road. That was the story of the Joad family, those country people driven off their land and carrying inside their shells the seeds of their own worth, crossing the country to California, hill-billy sucker bait for hustlers and troopers and goon squads, but surviving and disappearing down some dust road.

There is always that writer who seems, when you are young, to have caught hold of life as you feel it. Suddenly people in the streets, their eyes and the shape of their mouths, tell you stories. What I saw in the streets of the city I carry with me, my own city, so different from Steinbeck's California, were men and women standing in their own graves. I don't know why. That's what their faces told me. But I suffered no depression, I always believed that making her way down Yonge Street was Rose of Sharon, her child born dead and her breasts full of milk, and at the end, she would take some man's head, some man unable to feed himself, and nurse him as a child. I've argued with men of refinement about that scene. Crude, they called it. Crude and melodramatic and cheap. Of course, they admired Henry James, fussing and fidgeting in their own lives, incapable of large gestures, suffocating in circularities of prose. Those circularities told their own, more careful truth. I was too young to be careful.

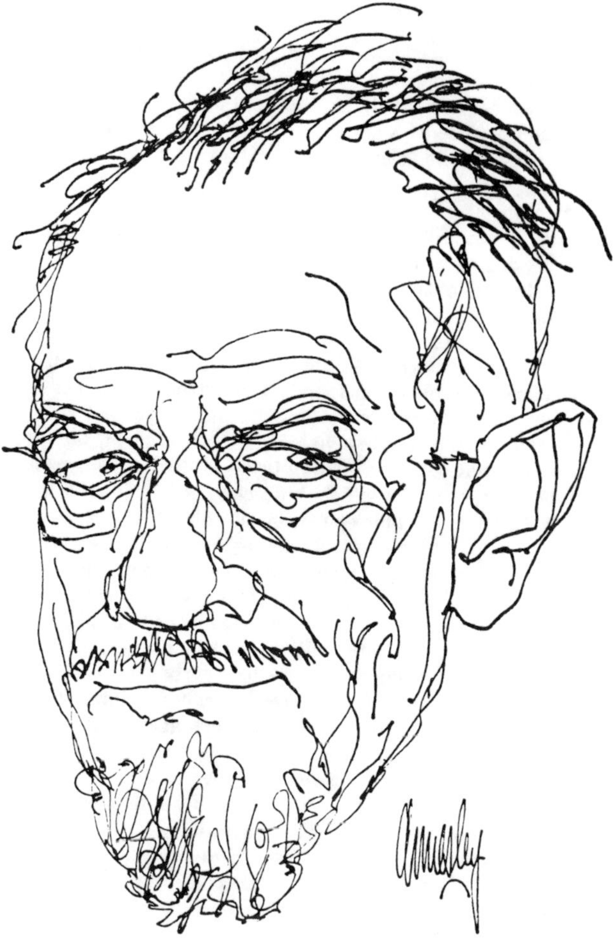

As for *Of Mice and Men:* I remember sitting in a bar on Bloor Street with a girl younger than I was, and I wanted her to love me so much that I swarmed all over her with affection and slowly she disappeared, terrified and bewildered, sinking down into her chair and I knew I was losing her, but I didn't understand why, and so I poured my feelings upon her.

Later, when I read the story of big dumb Lennie in *Of Mice and Men,* petting his mouse or a puppy, brimming with the strength of his affection, his dreams of childish pleasures, I understood how dangerous demonstrations of love are. Lennie always killed the things he loved – and finally he strangled the daughter-in-law of his employer – and his friend George was obliged to shoot him to keep him from being lynched. All the powerful yearning of people was in Lennie, the terror of loneliness and the compulsion to love, so inarticulate yet so overwhelming; and it was after reading that story that I felt for the first time I'd lived for a long year, because I knew I'd again, and probably again scare those I wanted to love. I believed in Rose of Sharon and the beauty of her gesture. I hated the nit-pickers, the defensive little squibs who never came out of their pin-stripe postures. But there was Lennie, unaware in his largeness, and murderous in his purity. I learned to fear the pure of heart. I learned to fear what was best in myself.

This was the great thing about Steinbeck as a writer, at least as I read him as a young man. He succeeded in giving shape to all my emotions. I found that I saw life in terms of his stories. When wiser men dismissed Steinbeck as heavy-handed, limited in his view of human behavior, and clumsy in the construction of his novels, I was angry. Once, standing in my father's kitchen, he tried to convince me that Flaubert was the real writer and I brushed aside Madame Bovary as a silly broad and gave him a lecture on violence, survival, big business and humble virtues, and on and on, and at last he said, 'That's beautiful, that one writer should do all that for you ... that's what writing should be ... but you'll discover that there are more beasts than turtles in this world.'

I suppose the last time that Steinbeck seemed a shaping part of my life was when I had turned about 20 and was home from college. My brother had taken me around to one of his haunts for a pre-Christmas drink. Some men I'd met once or twice before came in and sat down, and one fell face-first into his oyster soup and waiters carried him out through the kitchen. A tall blonde, aloof but smiling, had come in with them carrying a frozen turkey on her shoulder, and she sat at the table with the turkey. She had an independent gaiety about her and so I joined the group and bored in on her to discover she was in love with Steinbeck's *The Pearl.* We talked and talked about Steinbeck and six years later, Steinbeck having brought us together, I married her.

Last night, having another pre-Christmas drink, I was told that Steinbeck was dead. I had not read him for years. His last novel, *The Winter Of Our Discontent,* was a terrible failure for me and I've not been able to bring myself to re-read the good old books. He had, in recent years, become a Viet Nam hawk, and I suppose if I re-read *The Grapes of Wrath* now, I'd see clearly that it was not a radical book at all. Steinbeck didn't really want to change anything. It would be like visiting an old school girl friend; all the fine feeling and energy of those years would be lost in a figure turned dumpy a decade later. So, Steinbeck remains in my mind as the writer who excited me with his words when I was young – when I didn't care about quibbles and when I wanted a book to move me, or forget it. I guess I'm older and wiser now, and shortly I'll find myself admiring Henry James (it's the fate of those in their thirties), but Steinbeck's death has cut away something, cut away those young years, walking excitedly through the streets, discovering in the faces of people histories of love and pain, spearhead seeds by the side of the road.

James T. Farrell

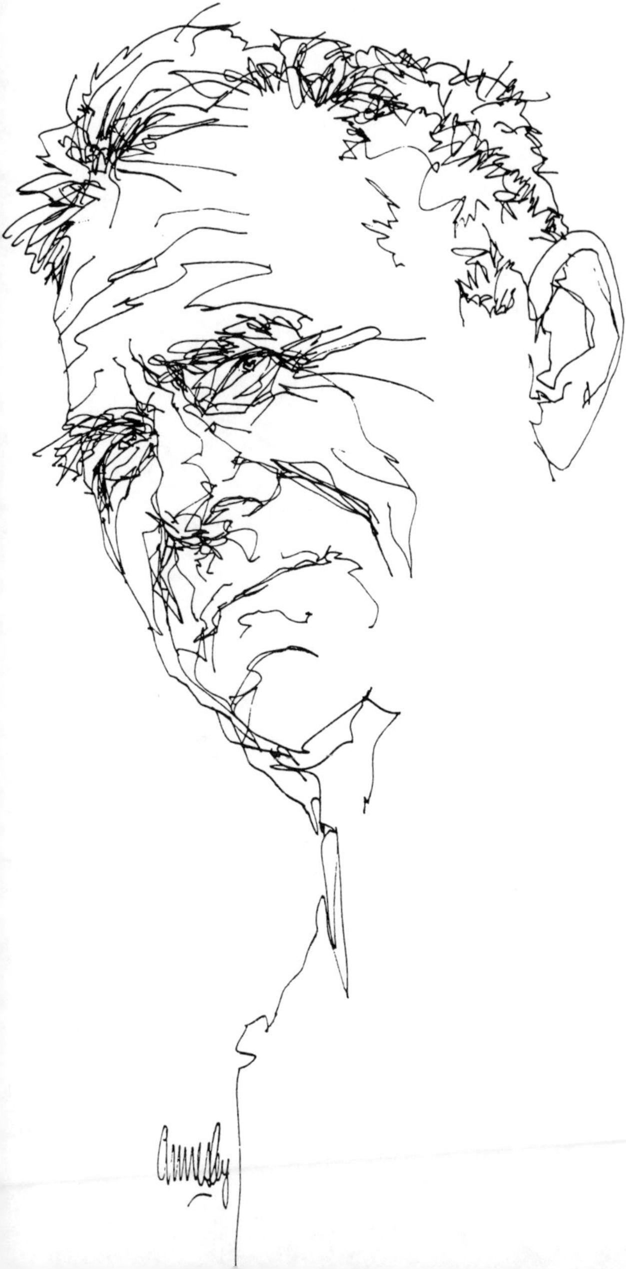

Tom Wolfe

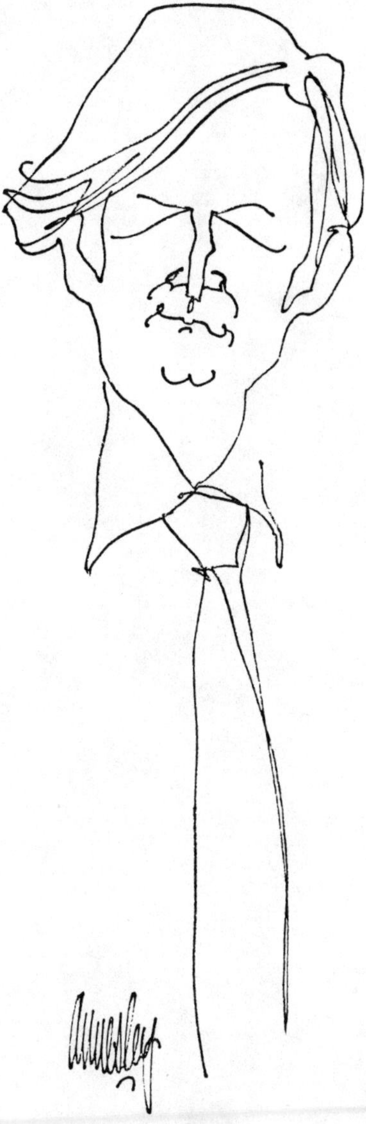

Raymond Massey

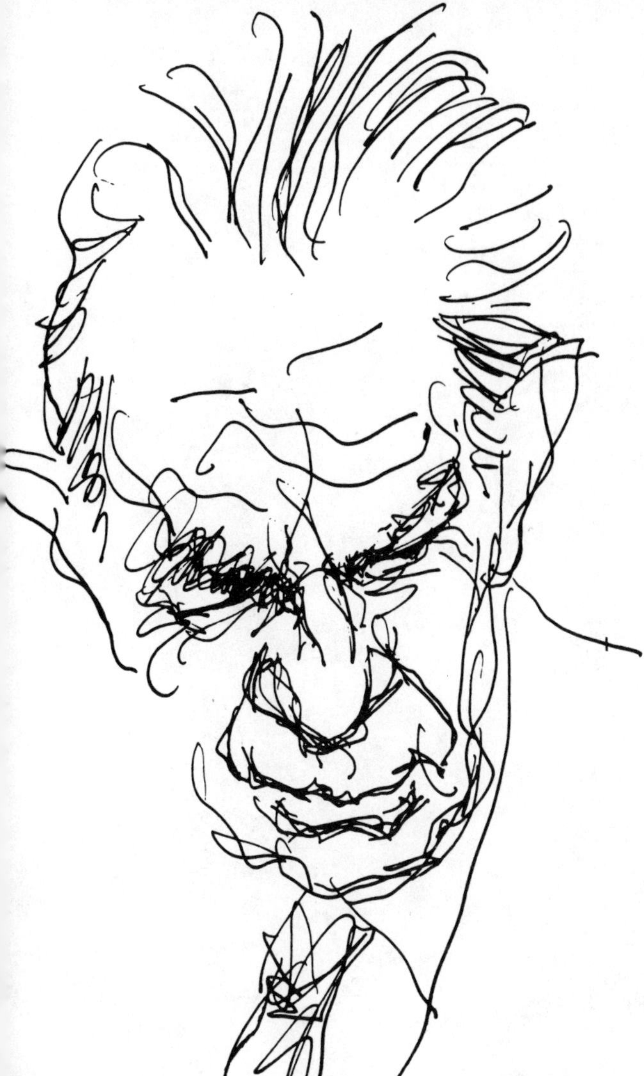

Lester Pearso

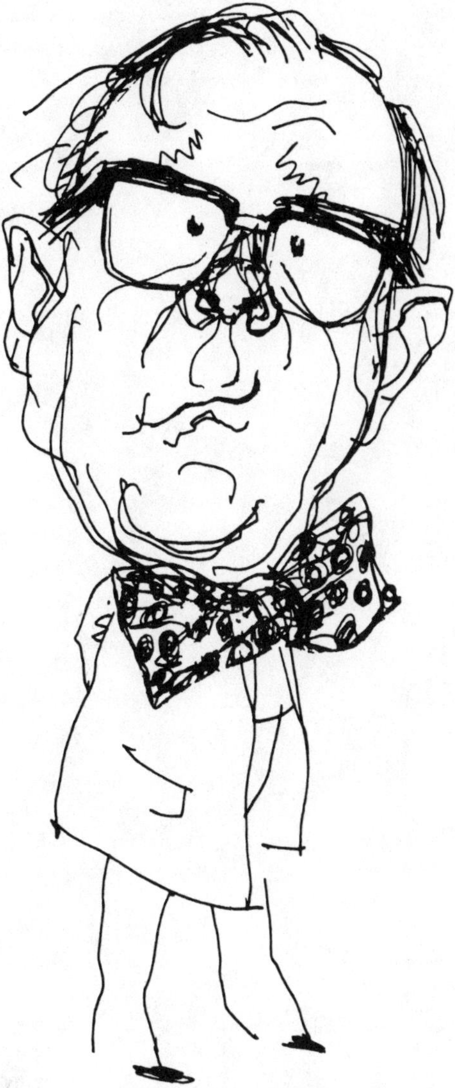

Tommy Douglas

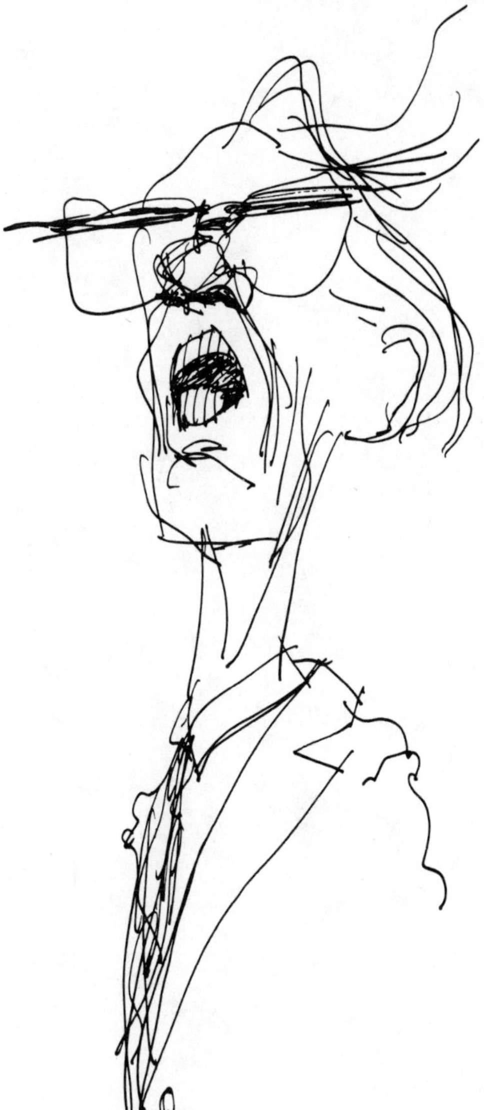

John Diefenbaker

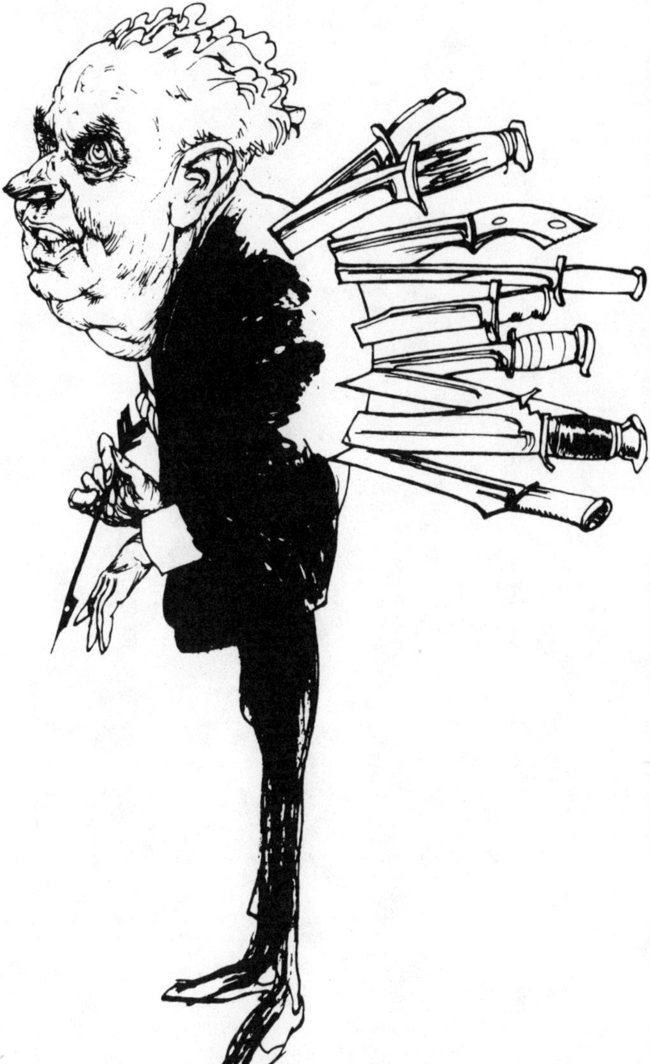

Margaret Atwood

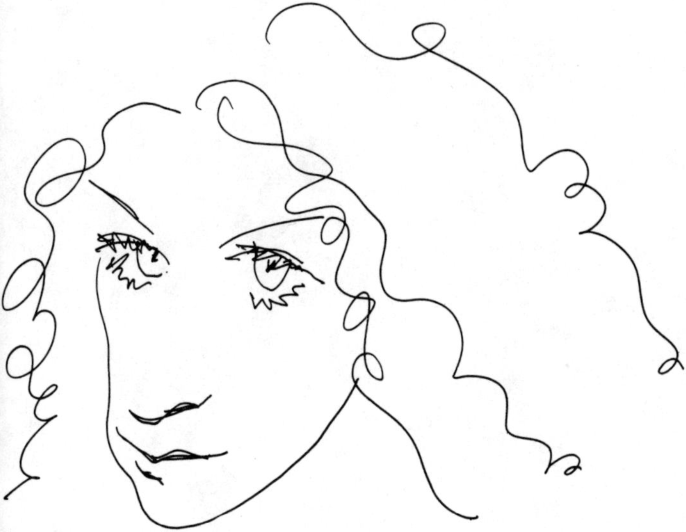

Stephen Leacock

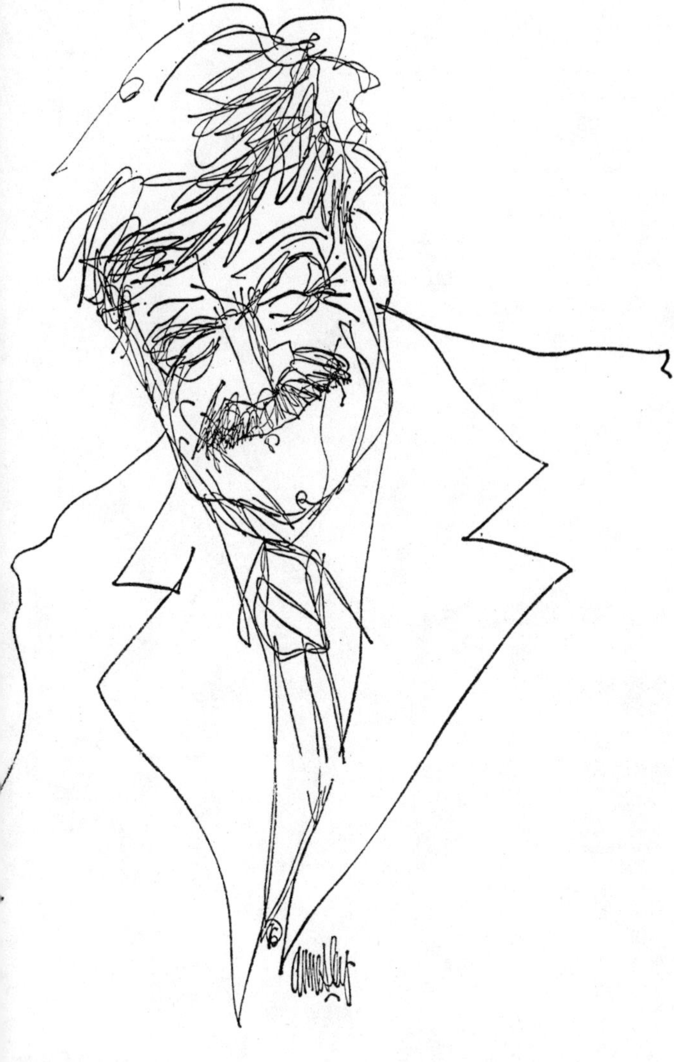

Hugh Garner

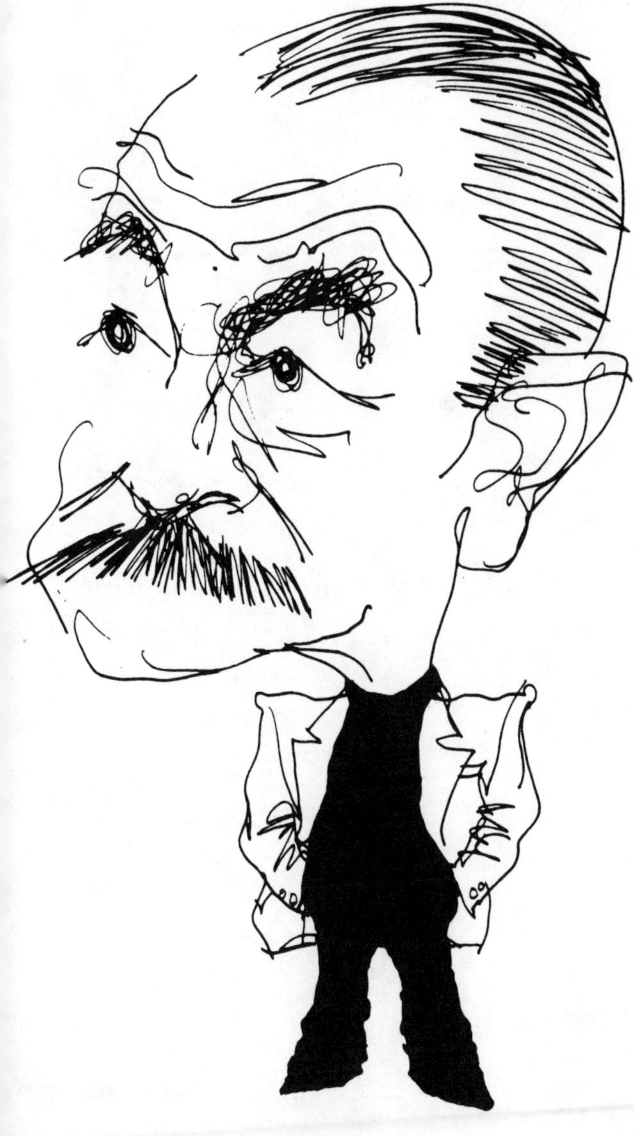

Frederick Phillip Grov

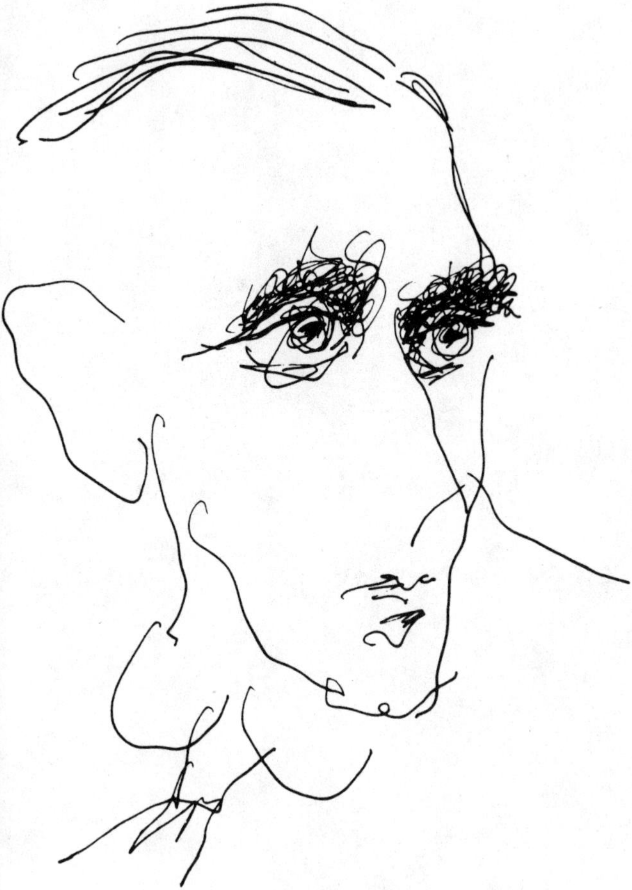

Al Purdy

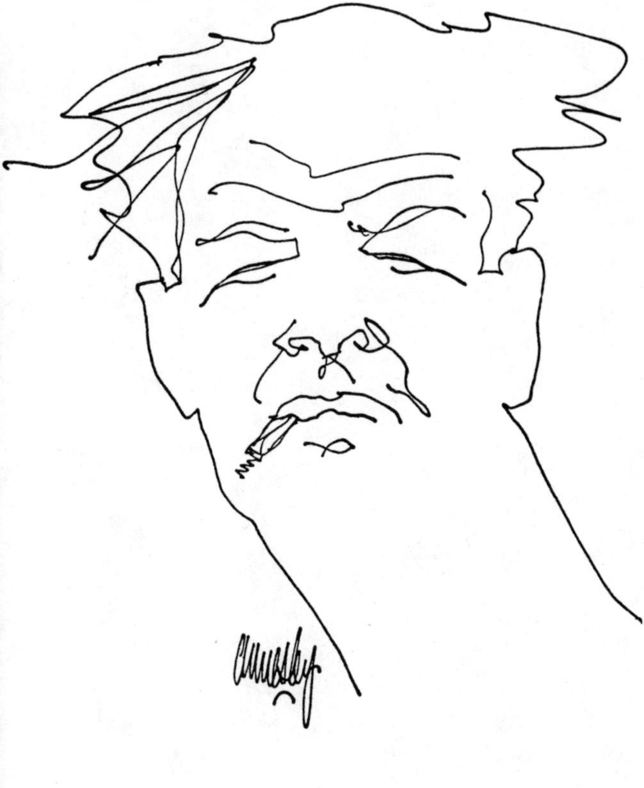

Edward R. Murrow

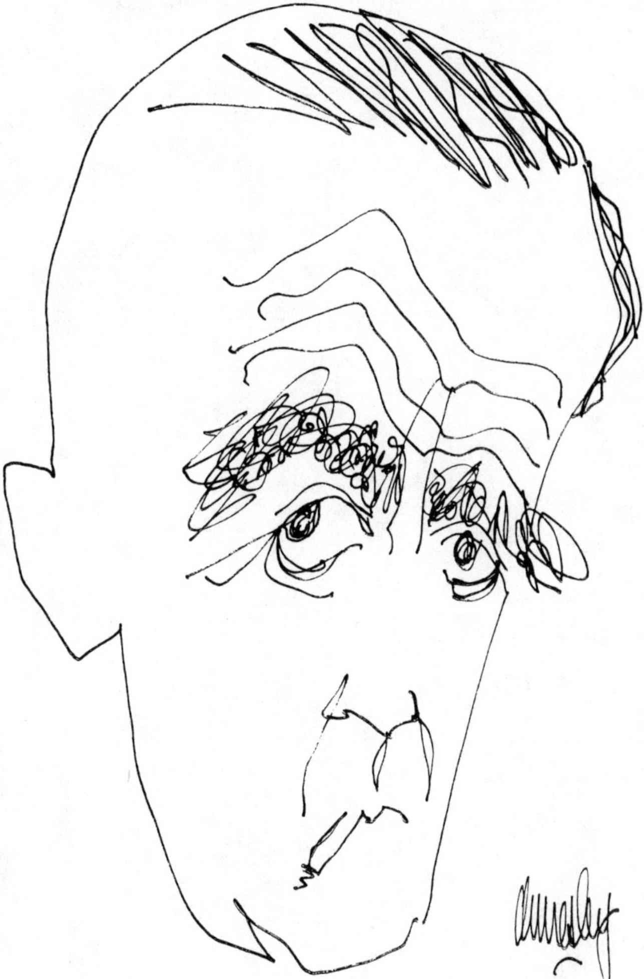

Dalton Camp

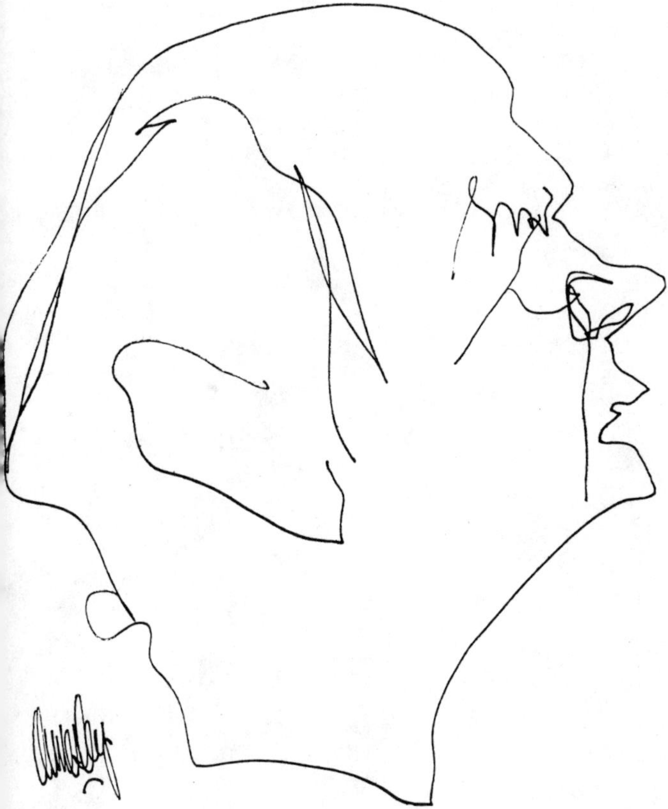

John Kenneth Galbraith

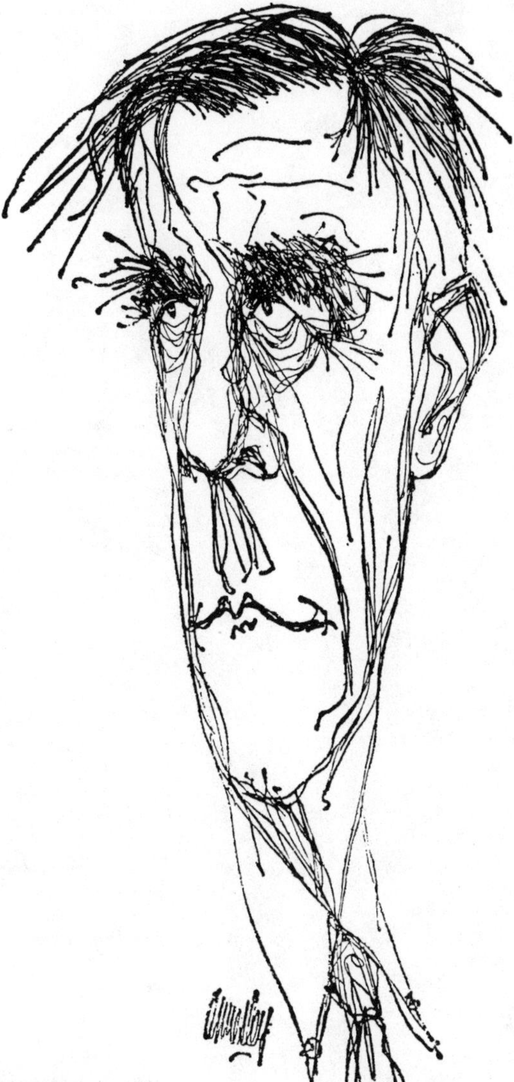

Marshall McLuhan

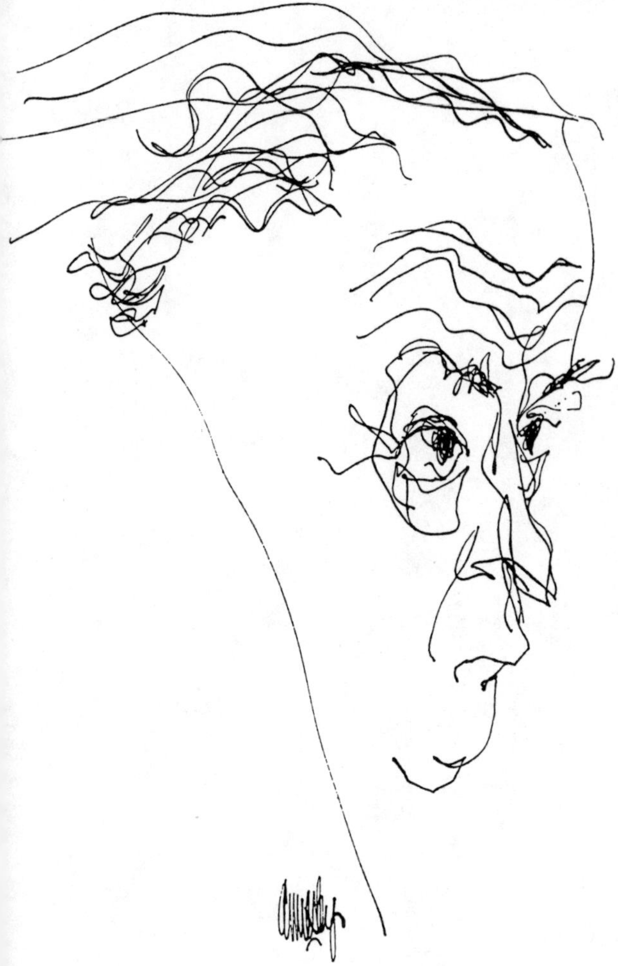

Farley Mowat

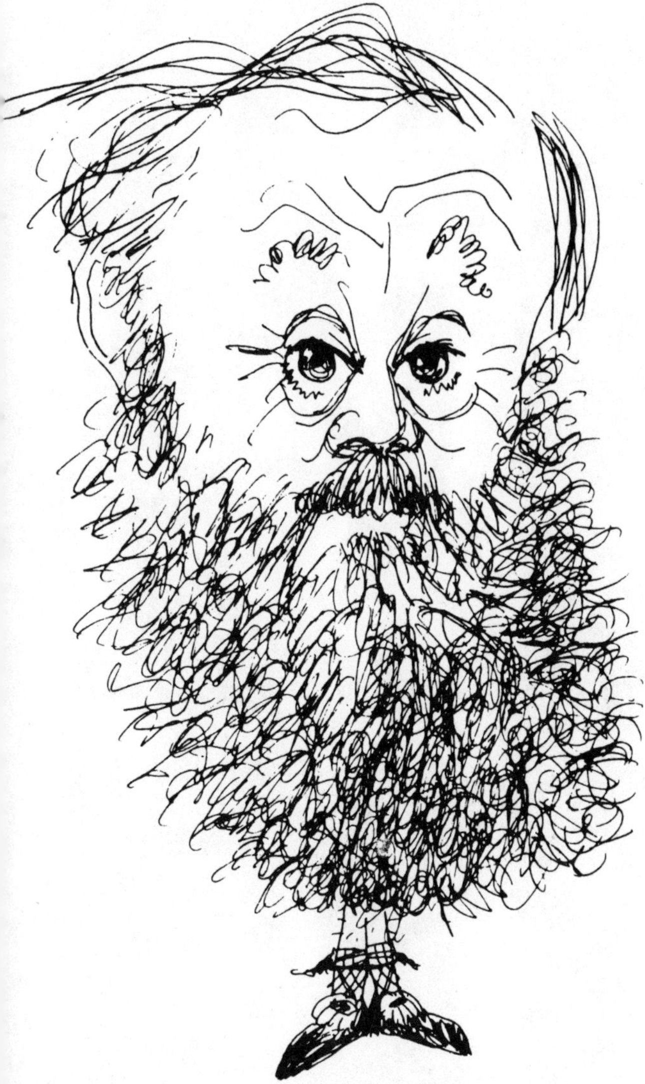

Larry Zolf

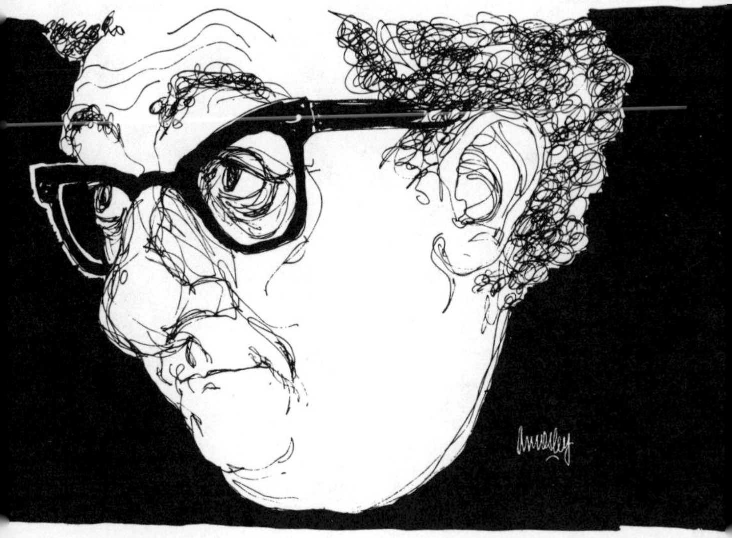